SO SORRY!
YOU'RE NOT GOING
TO SAVE IT

Brian Cockell

Copyright

Brian Cockell
website at www.thenarrowway.ca
Printed in the United States of America
First Printing: Jan 2022
ISBN 978-1-7771118-6-1

Table of Contents

DEDICATION

I dedicated this book to my extraordinary Editor Fonda, who also happens to be my loving wife and partner in Christ. Without her love, patience, support and hard work, this book would be less than it is, full of typos, misused words, and scattered thoughts. Thank you with all my love!

With honourable mention to my brother in Christ Torsten Schulz for his encouragement and support. Your love for the Lord is an inspiration and example for me to strive for daily.

PREFACE

The year was 2017. I fulfilled the role of Chief Operating Officer of one of Canada's largest private companies. Surrounded by corporate corruption, greed, and moral decay daily, I came to realize my life choices were not aligning with my Christian faith and the values and morals I held.

Fonda, my wife, and I lived on a 100-acre farm during this period. As a hobby, we ran a home-based skincare business, raised goats protected by 8 Maremma sheepdogs, and ran a bee apiary to create goat's milk and beeswax for the products we sold.

Fonda and I both decided enough was enough. We found ourselves firmly rooted in the world. Although we deeply loved the Lord, spent hours a day in the Word, prayed, went to church weekly, preached, and led a weekly bible study in our home, we knew we had to make a change. We firmly believe that we are in the season of our Lord's return for his church when we consider the words of scripture.

Matthew 25:21 *"His master replied, 'Well done, good and faithful servant! You have been faithful with a few things; I will put you in charge of many things. Come and share your master's happiness!"*

We asked ourselves, "When we stand before the Lord will we hear the words 'Well done, good and faithful servant'"? Our answer was no!

It was time to make the change we both knew we needed and required. We had to remove both feet from the world and dive headfirst into our faith and dedication to our Lord. Our desire and calling were to serve Jesus and enter the ministry. We did not know what that looked like at the time. However, Fonda and I left our jobs, sold most of our possessions, sold our farm, and moved off-the-grid to an unorganized territory in the deep North of Ontario. Today, 2021, we continue to run our skincare business from the bush, and our eight puppies are now pets rather than working dogs.

You have the culmination and result of the above changes in our life in your hands. This work is my second book and the continuation of my journey to teach and preach God's Word in this world that is now void of God and marching towards destruction and the end of days. May you be blessed, and may your faith and dedication to Jesus Christ be strengthened because of it.

A servant of Jesus Christ,
Brian Cockell

INTRODUCTION

Why did I write this book? Why should you have any interest in this book?

The Earth is experiencing climate change and global warming, earthquakes, floods, tsunamis, droughts, wildfires, natural disasters, environmental degradation, a depleting ozone layer, greenhouse gas emissions, pestilence, disease, famine, etc. and much more at an alarmingly accelerating rate. We see shorelines eroding, wild animal habitats drastically reducing through forestation and fire, the distinction of species, the melting of the polar ice caps, and the warming of our oceans.

The above list only scratches the surface of some of the issues we are currently facing on this planet. There are a whole host of new problems and dangers we are now aware of and also face from outer space and our solar system. Solar flares threatening our infrastructure, doomsday comets or asteroids on a potential collision course with the Earth, the wobbling of the Earth in its orbit, a decreasing magnet field of the planet, and this list goes on as well.

We also witness overpopulation, ongoing severe crop failures worldwide, species mutations from fertilization and chemical exposures, the devastation of the worldwide bee populations, the continuation of non-sustainable farming and agricultural practices, mega swarms of birds and locusts obliterating our food crops, killer bee and hornet swarms on the rise, the beginnings of ecological and societal collapse, and this list could go on forever.

Reading through the above three paragraphs paints a bleak picture of our current state of affairs. It is enough to send one into a deep depression or even wonder what the point of continuing on is. How has the human race possibly brought our planet to the brink of destruction in our short, chaotic history inhabiting what was once a majestic, beautiful planet? Are we to blame? Or is there something else cooking that escapes our notice, our thought, or even our intellects?

How do we know we face all the issues above? Are the problems above new problems that have only developed recently, or have they been growing since the beginning of the Industrial Revolution in the mid-1700s, or even possibly before that time? We know about these issues because the people who think they are the intelligent folks tell us so; the Scientists, Politicians, and the World Elites. Unfortunately, these folks are really not all that bright. Actually, they are, for the most part, self-serving idiots and not nearly as bright as they suppose they are.

"Woo, Brian," slow down, you say. That is no way for a Christian to address others. Yes, you are correct. Please accept my apology. I will readdress these folks using the scriptural words, the words of Christ himself, for self-focused, puffed up, God rejecting hypocrites. I will refer to them as a brood of vipers and evildoers instead. So there we go. That sounds like a much better description for them. What was once actual science is now politicized propaganda. Politics has now morphed into totalitarianism, stripping populations of civil liberties and religious freedoms. The global elites have moved out of the shadows and into the mainstream with loud, authoritative voices directing governments, media outlets, and the population down the path of their globalist agenda.

This group of three is hellbent on what they call "The Great Reset" of society into their vision of a one-world totalitarian government, of course, overseen and run by them. In actuality, they are puppets of the Devil doing his bidding as we march towards the great tribulation. They are deceivers who have been deceived into believing the lies of the Evil One and are marching the world to its ultimate doom. I cover these topics in my upcoming book, "Tribulation Training – Goats to the Left – Sheep to the right." As we move through this book, I will now refer to this group of three as the "Puppets" for brevity.

Several things need to happen for these Puppets of Satan to achieve their world domination and control agendas. First and foremost, the population needs to relinquish their civil liberties, freedoms, and religion needs to go away or be severely suppressed and marginalized. How will and do the

Puppets achieve this? Their primary tool is creating fear and fabricating life-threatening events for the populous—you and me. Once people and the world are cowering in fear of what is afoot, the saviours can then come to the rescue. These saviours are, of course, these Puppets of Satan.

Listening to today's propaganda, oops, I mean media, one would think and assume we only have a year or two if we are lucky before we doom our planet and ourselves to ultimate destruction. Oh no! What is going to get us? Is it global warming, climate change, or natural disasters caused by our flagrant consumption of resources? Maybe it will be a pandemic or the depletion of our ozone layer from the gases we release into the atmosphere, or a cosmic event from our solar system. Perhaps we might all starve to death or be obliterated by nuclear annihilation. Or maybe it will be one of the other umpteen disasters they have devised for us. I am taking bets on none of the above. We are indeed headed for the destruction of this planet, however, on God's terms and according to His plans. The Puppets have no say in the matter of the when and how. This is where this book will take us.

In the Bible, we are given the responsibility of being good stewards of and exercising dominion over the Earth, as we read in Genesis 1:26-28.

(Genesis 1:26-28)
Then God said, "Let Us (Father, Son, Holy Spirit) make man in Our image, according to Our likeness [not physical, but a spiritual personality and moral likeness]; and let them have complete authority over the fish of the sea, the birds of the air, the cattle, and over the entire earth, and over everything that creeps and crawls on the earth." So God created man in His own image, in the image and likeness of God He created him; male and female He created them. And God blessed them [granting them certain authority] and said to them, "Be fruitful, multiply, and fill the earth, and subjugate it [putting it under your power]; and rule over (dominate) the fish of the sea, the birds of the air, and every living thing that moves upon the earth." (AMP)

Should we be polluting, abusing or treating the planet irresponsibly, as is our habit? No, of course, we should not; however, we are found guilty as charged; that's on us. This failing on the part of humanity, as sad as it is, does not have any effect on the planet's ultimate demise. The Puppets attempting to convince you otherwise, shouting at the top of their lungs, are full of lies, misdirection and deception. Cutting down trees, driving to work, and spraying some aerosol cans is not going to knock our planet out of its orbit and send us all on a collision course to our doom – period. However, we are heading to the end, just not how you might think or are being told.

Throughout this book, I will endeavour to sift through the lies and deceptions from what we are told. We will debunk most of the crap being spewed and be left with the actual truth of the matter at hand. Are there fundamental problems as described above? Sure there are. Are they from the causes the Puppets are selling you? No, they are not, for the most part. I will detail from a biblical perspective how we have ended up where we are and where we are actually going to arrive at being the ultimate end of this world as we know it. It will come about very differently than what the Puppets are telling you.

IN THE BEGINNING

The very first verse of the Bible, the book of Genesis, describes the creation of this world. In the second verse, God describes the initial state of the world after He created it.

(Genesis 1)
"In the beginning God created the heavens and the Earth. Now the Earth was formless and empty, darkness was over the surface of the deep, and the Spirit of God was hovering over the waters."

In the beginning, as God describes the creation of the heavens and the Earth, is a great place to start. The first defence of my opening statements and denial of the narratives being thrown at us by the Puppets of the Devil is to Biblically prove that God is in control of His creation, not man. God and God alone will ultimately determine when this Earth expires and how. It is God who holds this Earth in place and sustains all living things in it, including you and me, as we read in Hebrews 1:3.

(Hebrews 1:3)

"The Son is the radiance and only expression of the glory of [our awesome] God [reflecting God's Shekinah glory, the Light-being, the brilliant light of the divine], and the exact representation and perfect imprint of His [Father's] essence, and upholding and maintaining and propelling all things [the entire physical and spiritual universe] by His powerful word [carrying the universe along to its predetermined goal]. When He [Himself and no other] had [by offering Himself on the cross as a sacrifice for sin] accomplished purification from sins and established our freedom from guilt, He sat down [revealing His completed work] at the right hand of the Majesty on high [revealing His Divine authority]," (AMP)

My goal has always been to write in a relatively simplistic manner and communicate my thoughts clearly. My goal is not to glorify myself or sound intelligent but to glorify God and help further His Kingdom. However, every once in a while, I need to rely on a bit of science to communicate an intended thought. This opening defence is one of those times but stick with me. It will be worth it.

The first issue with taking direction and advice from the Puppets is they are God-haters and rejecters, mockers and scoffers. That alone should be enough to understand that a significant problem develops from the message's origin alone. They deny the Divine authority of God, and they reject Him in general. They certainly reject God as the creator of all things and that He is in complete control.

(Isaiah 48:13)
"My own hand laid the foundations of the earth, and my right hand spread out the heavens; when I summon them, they all stand up together."

These Puppets rely on the propagandized science they have created to move their message forward without relying on or understanding actual science. If they took the time to understand what fundamental science looked like, they would have no choice but to recognize a God of Divine nature and authority. The God of the Bible exists outside of time, space and matter. If He did not, he would not be God but rather just another being like you and me inside the creation and certainly not worthy of our worship. God exists and is sustained in and of himself outside of time, space and matter. God gave us these three elements of time, space, and matter at the world's creation.

(Genesis 1)
"In the beginning **{Time}** *God created the heavens* **{Space}** *and the earth* **{Matter}**. *Now the Earth was formless and empty, darkness was over the surface of the deep, and the Spirit of God was hovering over the waters."* *{Emphasis added}*

All three of these elements are necessary for our existence, and all three need to come into existence at the exact same time and coexist, which of course, debunks the big bang theory as a fairy-tale. Where would you put it if you have time and matter but no space? When would you put it without time if you only had matter and space? There would be nothing in it if you just had space and time without matter. All three coexist in a trinity just like our triune God exists in the Trinity of Father, Son, Spirit. Each of these elements on its own has a triune aspect. Time is past, present and future. Space is length, width, and height. Matter is solid, liquid, and gas. God's first act of creation was to bring these three elements into existence as he created the heavens and the Earth, and He has bound us within these three constraints. There is no escaping either one of them.

On the other hand, God is in no way bound by his creation or affected by time, space, or matter; instead, he sustains it by his Word and Divine power, as we read in Hebrews 1:3 above. The arrogance of man and, in particular, these Puppets, to imagine God is not in control and ordering his creation as he sees fit is astounding. One day they each will stand before the Almighty God to give an account, and it will not go well for them. Unfortunately, we are stuck with their false narratives and misguided, self-serving actions that affect all of us until then.

To consider a simplistic, real-world example of the concept of time, space, and matter and how God is separate from them, consider the book that is in your hands. The time is now; you are reading it. The matter is the book itself. The space is the book between your hands. Although all three of these statements are accurate and valid, you could not have one element without the other. You could change the elements around by putting the book on the table, but you still have the space in which it resides. It is simply a different space – on the table.

The book's creator is not in the book or moving letters around and turning pages. He exists outside of the book's time, space, and matter and is probably having a nice afternoon nap right about now. Chuckle. To presuppose God does not exist or is not in ultimate control exercising His divine authority over his creation is the first major mistake of the Puppets that completely nullifies their ridiculous narratives of destruction and doom and gloom they are spewing.

We do not need the Puppets or their agendas to save us; we should probably leave that to God and our relationship with him. If you don't have a relationship with God, you should probably establish one quickly. More on this later in the book. As I stated in a rather harsh manner in the opening, they are really not all that bright. They are a bunch of bumbling idiots running around puffing themselves up to themselves and each other at our expense. Darn, I did it again. Sorry.

To summarize the above thoughts and truth, God alone is in control of his creation. He alone will determine what course his creation takes and when this world as we know it comes to an end. We can do nothing as His created to alter the path that God has predetermined for this world, independent of what the Puppets are telling us. We are ultimately heading to the destruction and end of this planet when God tells us and when He has determined. Anyone who tells you differently is sadly deluded. The Puppets have or are themselves being deceived. They are led around by the nose by that great deceiver we know as Satan, the Devil, the god of this world.

Although these supposed smart folks have it wrong, we are still left with the problem of our world quickly spinning into oblivion. If they do not, who does have the correct answer to our current plight? God, of course, and He spells out the path of humanity with a detailed road map that we are following. As we are exploring, we are told what our path and end will be at the beginning of the scriptures.

In the beginning, on the 6th day of creation, God created Adam and Eve from the dust of the Earth and breathed into their nostrils the breath of life.

(Genesis 2:7-8)
"Then the Lord God formed [that is, created the body of] man from the dust of the ground, and breathed into his nostrils the breath of life; and the man became a living being [an individual complete in body and spirit]. And the Lord God planted a garden (oasis) in the east, in Eden (delight, land of happiness); and He put the man whom He had formed (created) there." (AMP)

Adam and Eve were without sin and walked in fellowship with God in the garden of Eden. Most, whether Christian or not, know the story. Amid the garden, God planted the Tree of Life (To grant or sustain eternal life, Genesis 3:22), and the tree known as the tree of the knowledge of good and evil. Many other trees were planted that provided food for Adam and Eve.

(Genesis 1:9)

"And [in that garden] the Lord God caused to grow from the ground every tree that is desirable and pleasing to the sight and good (suitable, pleasant) for food; the tree of life was also in the midst of the garden, and the tree of the [experiential] knowledge (recognition) of [the difference between] good and evil." (AMP)

The setting God created for Adam and Eve was a blissful paradise greater than any place we could possibly imagine. God provided for all their needs and walked with them in fellowship. They only knew good; evil and disobedience had not yet been introduced to them. As stated earlier, they were without sin and, at this point, eternal beings. Their purpose was to fellowship with God and tend to the garden he had created for them. The curse of death and the curse of the Earth had not yet entered into our history.

(Genesis 1:16-17)
And the Lord God commanded the man, saying, "You may freely (unconditionally) eat [the fruit] from every tree of the garden; but [only] from the tree of the knowledge (recognition) of good and evil you shall not eat, otherwise on the day that

you eat from it, you shall most certainly die [because of your disobedience].”

God placed the forbidden tree, the tree of the knowledge of good and evil, in the garden with explicit instructions. Do not eat of it—many wonder why it was placed there in the first place. The tree demonstrates the free will God created us with as one reason. Adam had a choice. To eat of the tree or not to eat of it.

The tree's existence within the garden is where our story starts to take a wrong turn. God tells Adam that he would certainly die if he ate from this particular tree. God is not referring to an instant death but an ultimate physical death that he was currently not subject to as an eternal being. Ultimate physical death would be Adam's price for disobeying God by eating from the tree. Shortly after Adam's direction from God, Satan shows up to spew his lies and deceit to Eve.

(Genesis 3:2-5)
“And the woman said to the serpent, ‘We may eat of the fruit of the trees in the garden, but God said, ‘You shall not

eat of the fruit of the tree that is in the midst of the garden, neither shall you touch it, lest you die.'" But the serpent said to the woman, "You will not surely die. For God knows that when you eat of it your eyes will be opened, and you will be like God, knowing good and evil." (ESV)

Ultimately, after being deceived with lies from Satan, Eve took and ate of the fruit, gave some to Adam, and he ate of it as well. The story of humankind now takes a dark turn, leading ultimately to where we are today. The purpose of this book is not to write an apologetic on the first chapter of Genesis. The beginning of our story walks us to the point of understanding how we have ended up in the state we are in today as a people and what is happening to our planet. After eating the fruit, God now places curses on humankind and His creation as a penalty for this disobedience to Him. This brings us to the true reason for our state and the world's decay.

After Adam and Eve have eaten from the tree of the knowledge of good and evil, God approaches each participant and pronounces judgement on them for their disobedience to Him.

(Genesis 1:14-15)

So the Lord God said to the serpent, "Because you have done this, "Cursed are you above all livestock and all wild animals! You will crawl on your belly and you will eat dust all the days of your life. And I will put enmity between you and the woman, and between your offspring and hers; he will crush your head, and you will strike his heel."

(Genesis 1:16)

"I will make your pains in childbearing very severe; with painful labor you will give birth to children. Your desire will be for your husband, and he will rule over you."

(Genesis 1:17-18)

To Adam he said, "Because you listened to your wife and ate fruit from the tree about which I commanded you, 'You must not eat from it,' "Cursed is the ground because of you; through painful toil you will eat food from it all the days of your life. It will produce thorns and thistles for you, and you will eat the plants of the field. By the sweat of your brow you will eat your food until you return to the ground, since from it you were taken; for dust you are and to dust you will return."

Disobedience and rebellion against God come at a grave price. Adam and Eve lived in an unimaginable eternal paradise, fellowshipping and walking with God. There was no sorrow, sickness, pestilence, environmental upheaval, drought, famine, or any of the woes we face today. God provided all their needs, and the work of tending the garden was a rewarding joy. They were without sin and walked blameless before God. The planet was without blemish or decay and considered, in all things, good, as described by God throughout the creation days.

(Genesis 1:31)
"God saw all that he had made, and it was very good. And there was evening, and there was morning—the sixth day."

Once Eve was deceived by the Devil, that serpent of old we call Satan, ate the forbidden fruit and subsequently offered it to Adam, and he ate, everything came crashing down around them. God now pronounces the judgement on each one of them, as we see above. The curse Adam received was most grievous and set a new course for humankind that has been passed down to all generations, as we see in Romans 5:12 to name one of many similar passages.

(Romans 5:12)
"Therefore, just as sin entered the world through one man, and death through sin, and in this way death came to all people, because all sinned—"

Adam went from being an eternal being without sin, fellowshipping and walking with God, to being outcast from the garden and separated from his creator due to his disobedience or sin. He would now have to work a blighted land with thorns and thistles by the sweat of his brow in painful toil all of his days separate from God and, ultimately, experience physical death. As we see in Romans 5:12, the curse God placed on Adam and the land has been passed to every subsequent generation since, including you and me.

We now come to the topic at hand; the Earth and the curse placed upon it. When God placed the curse on the Earth, it went from an eternal paradise to a temporal home full of blight and decay. Decay was introduced to humankind, the Earth, and all

God had created. No longer was God's creation considered good in his eyes. Adam, through his disobedience, changed the course of the path our destiny would take.

The introduction of decay into God's creation drastically changes the narrative from one of eternal contentment before and with God, on the planet and in the solar system he made for us to one of tragedy and calamity for us and the world. The Good news is. God left us an out, which we will look at later in the book.

What is this decay? One of the best ways to understand the curse or decay God imposed on his creation is to look at one of its definitions. Decay can be defined as a gradual falling into an inferior condition or progressive decline. Everything God created is now cursed with progressive decline, meaning it ultimately suffers a slow death. You, me, the Earth, the solar system and everything in it. Nothing escapes God's judgment, and no one other than God has the ability to change this fact, especially the Puppets and their vain scheming to do so.

Rather than removing the curse, God has chosen to develop a new plan. A plan for our redemption through His Son for our salvation. God's new plan provides a new heaven and a new earth for those who put their faith and belief in Jesus Christ, His Son. We will discuss this in detail in a later chapter. For now, we will continue to concentrate on the fate of this Earth.

It is not too hard to figure out where we are going. The Puppets at least have this part correct, albeit for all the wrong reasons and with all the false solutions. The planet is doomed for two reasons, scientific evidence of constant decay unto destruction, and more importantly, God says it is on its way out and soon. There is nothing you or the Puppets can do about it. God has foreordained it; the destruction will happen as God has decreed and scheduled according to His time. These evil Puppets have no say in the matter. As a matter of fact, God sits back and laughs at their foolishness.

(Psalm 37:13)

"but the Lord laughs at the wicked, for he knows their day is coming."

As we travel through the book, we will debunk a number of claims the elites, those evil, wicked, Puppets of Satan, are making through Biblical study of the topics and scientific actualities recorded through history. Through this scriptural and scientific analysis, I will demonstrate both the error of the Puppets and the truth of the scriptural account of the past, present and what the future holds. The Word is clear, unambiguous, and without error or contradiction. What God decrees comes to pass. Let's dig a little deeper.

THE PUPPETS

We defined the Puppets as Government, Scientists, and Global Elites, all beholden to and following the agenda of the Devil. To better clarify the roles of each, the majority of those we call scientists have forsaken investigatory application of subject matters to parroting what they are told to by the Elites and the Governments. The Elites and Governments use a beholden Media to deliver their mandates and Globalizing agendas through the fear they propagate. Ok, that is a little more clarifying.

What is it that they are actually propagating and telling us to Fear? Let's start with some history in this chapter and then we will dig into each item and debunk the lies, deception and falsehoods they are spewing. When listening to the new narrative, we first notice that it is no longer isolated to a particular group, region, city, state or country. A cohesive message is coming at us from all governments and nations worldwide. For the first time in our short history, a globalized agenda is emerging. Everyone appears to be on the same page and reading from the same playbook. How is this possible? It is something new to the world but should be no surprise to the student of the Bible.

To answer the question of how it has become possible that the world governments are all singing from the same playbook, we only need to look into history to find our answer of why and how. Back in and around 3500 to 3000 BC in the plain of Shinar, the folks, under Nimrod's leadership, began to build a tower to the height of the heavens. We call this tower the tower of Babel. At this point in our history, the world was of one language. When God looked down on their efforts, He was not pleased.

(Genesis 11:1-9)
Now the whole Earth spoke one language and used the same words (vocabulary). And as people journeyed eastward, they found a plain in the land of Shinar and they settled there. They said one to another, "Come, let us make bricks and fire them thoroughly [in a kiln, to harden and strengthen them]." So they used brick for stone [as building material], and they used tar (bitumen, asphalt) for mortar. They said, "Come, let us build a city for ourselves, and a tower whose top will reach into the heavens, and let us make a [famous] name for ourselves, so that we will not be scattered [into

separate groups] and be dispersed over the surface of the entire earth [as the Lord instructed]." Now the Lord came down to see the city and the tower which the sons of men had built. And the Lord said, "Behold, they are one [unified] people, and they all have the same language. This is only the beginning of what they will do [in rebellion against Me], and now no evil thing they imagine they can do will be impossible for them. Come, let Us (Father, Son, Holy Spirit) go down and there confuse and mix up their language, so that they will not understand one another's speech." So the Lord scattered them abroad from there over the surface of the entire Earth; and they stopped building the city. Therefore the name of the city was Babel—because there the Lord confused the language of the entire Earth; and from that place the Lord scattered and dispersed them over the surface of all the Earth." (AMP)

Alright, keep this story in mind for a second; we will be right back to it. We need to back up just a little further to understand God's disappointment with man's unrelenting sin and continual turning away from God. In Genesis 6:5-6, we see that God was witnessing the utter wickedness of man with nothing but evil in his heart all of his days. God was deeply troubled in his heart by what he was seeing and decided to wipe the world clean of these evildoers and start again with one soul and his family he found favour with – Noah. Que the flood.

(Genesis 6:5-6)
The Lord saw how great the wickedness of the human race had become on the Earth, and that every inclination of the thoughts of the human heart was only evil all the time.

After the flood event, Noah found favour in God's sight and was given the instructions to be fruitful and multiply, to increase in numbers and fill the Earth. There are a couple of things you will notice through the flood narrative that is worth pointing out. First, God alone determined what would happen with men and the Earth. Humankind had no say in the matter or the ability to reverse the course God had decided upon. The floodwaters were coming. The Puppets of Noah's day mocked and scoffed as Noah built the ark. We know how it ended for those scoffers.

The other very interesting thing of note is that God instructed Noah to repopulate and FILL the

Earth. He did not want humankind to congregate in a small geographical area. It was a new beginning for Noah and mankind. A reset, if you will; however, a reset determined by God alone. Not mankind.

(Genesis 9:1)
"Then God blessed Noah and his sons, saying to them, "Be fruitful and increase in number and fill the earth."

God then made a convenient with Noah. a commitment to maintain His relationship with mankind and never again destroy the Earth with a flood. This pledge, given unconditionally to Noah and all the living creatures on Earth, was accompanied by the sign of the rainbow. We can be sure water, the melting of the polar ice caps, or any weather event concerning water will not be our doom. How do we know that? Because God says so. The next time you see a rainbow, you can remind yourself of this fact. If anyone runs into any of the Puppets, let them know they are off-course on this one and point them to the Genesis narrative. The Earth will not meet its doom by global warming and the melting of the polar ice caps.

(Genesis 9:14-15)
"Whenever I bring clouds over the Earth and the rainbow appears in the clouds, I will remember my covenant between me and you and all living creatures of every kind. Never again will the waters become a flood to destroy all life."

With the above knowledge as a backdrop, back to our Tower of Babel discourse. The first thing the descendants of Noah decided upon, in direct rebellion against God's instructions, was not to disperse around or fill the Earth as commanded; mistake number one. Instead, they determined they would gather in the plain of Shinar.

Their rebellious act does not end there. Then these descendants of Noah decided to build a city with a tower that would reach the heavens. Their second mistake was not believing God that He would never destroy them by water again. They constructed their tower with waterproof materials assuming they would be protecting themselves from another flood extinction event.

God declares that when men get together to scheme, they can accomplish anything they set their evil minds on achieving. God says this is only the beginning of what they will do, and now no evil thing they imagine they can do will be impossible for them. Not a great commentary for the nature of man. Rather than let this rebellion stand, God decides to do for them what they rejected to do at his command. He scatters them across the face of the Earth and confuses their language so they cannot continue their unified scheming and disobedience against God. They were dispersed and given unique languages in each area God sent them to.

It is said, and with certainty, that history repeats itself. We have witnessed mankind returning to the same rebellion of Noah's descendants in the past century. We call it progress, modernization, and globalization. God calls it rebellion and evil hearts scheming. I ultimately realize how drastic of a statement that sounds like; however, I am positive God has not had a change of heart when it comes to his directives for mankind. At no point in the scriptures do we find permission to reassemble as one people under one language.

I hear you saying, "Brian, there are still distinct languages out there." Yes, you are correct; however, you and I can now communicate with anyone in the world in their language. Technology has provided us with in-time translators for speech and conversations and technology on the internet to transcribe any language into your language. Not only can we now communicate, but we can also hop on a plane and do it face to face. It sure sounds to me that we are reversing God's instructions and bringing ourselves back together as one globalized community and nation. We are not there yet, but it is just around the corner. The foundation is being set, so to speak.

God separated us and confused our languages by his providence and will. We have set God aside by our providence and will, claiming our own authority over our actions, setting aside accountability to God. Plus, the proof is in the pudding. The closer we become to uniting the world, the more egregious our ways become, exposing the true sinful nature of our hearts and actions led on by the Puppets. You don't have to look too far to see the evil afoot.

The third error of Noah's descendants was to conspire to build their tower to the heavens. Not only did they make the conscious decision to rebel against God's instructions, but they also conspired to seat themselves equal to and beside God. These actions sound somewhat familiar to another Biblical story of a created being seeking to be equal to or even greater than God. Satan desired to raise his throne above the stars of God and make himself like God.

(Isaiah 14:12-14)
"How you have fallen from heaven, morning star, son of the dawn! You have been cast down to the Earth, you who once laid low the nations! You said in your heart," "I will ascend to the heavens; I will raise my throne above the stars of God; I will sit enthroned on the mount of assembly, on the utmost heights of Mount Zaphon. I will ascend above the tops of the clouds; I will make myself like the Most High."

The first rebellion against God orchestrated by the Evil One ended up being the instigating incident that ultimately led to mankind's fall, introducing sin and death into our race and our separation from God. The Tower of Babel's rebellion led to God dispersing mankind throughout the Earth, confusing our languages.

It is safe to say that rebellion against God never goes well. Our current rebellion, repeating the history of these first events, will be the final event that ultimately leads to the end of this Earth as we know it ushering in the return of our Lord Jesus Christ. In no way can the Puppets or our actions change this course contrary to popular belief and what we are told. We will explore more on the Lord's return as we move through the book.

I find it extremely difficult to look at our modern society and at those who oversee and direct it, the Puppets, and try to imagine a reset that remains faithful to God's instructions and decrees. It can't and won't happen, which leaves us on our God-ordained course of reaching the end of these times. The Puppets are hellbent on mimicking all of the events that caused God to intervene in the plain of Shinar at the Tower of Babel. Once again, God will ultimately take direct action against the plans of men, as the Bible spells out in the end day events. These Puppets are executing their plan in place of God's, relegating him to the sidelines, or so they think.

Again, I hear you saying, "Brian, you're being a little extreme, aren't you?" Am I? I am not so sure. Our current course mimics the Babel event to a tee. What is it the Puppets are orchestrating for us, or better yet, them, to accomplish? God dispersed Noah's descendants for their own good. He saw that when we remain together as one, our hearts contrive only evil resulting in evil plans contrary to and in opposition to God and His plans. God dispersed them to suppress the evil within them that becomes more prominent when joined together as one for their own good.

The first action of Noah's descendants was to bring the people together, in the plain of Shinar, under the leadership of Nimrod. God said no and dispersed them. The first action of the Puppets in unison has been to reverse God's action and return all the people of the Earth back into one globalized nation. We know this globalized body and leadership, which will ultimately rule the world, will be run by one ruler we call the Antichrist supported by the False Prophet. (Topics I cover in my upcoming book: Tribulation Training – Goats to the Left, Sheep to the Right).

The second action of Noah's descendants was to construct a tower to the Heavens to seat themselves beside God. You don't have to look very far to see the enormous towers we now build to the heavens, with each nation vying to outdo the next to get there first. Sure, we don't acknowledge our goal is to reach God but rather attribute the construction feat of these towers to human ingenuity but ultimately, why? There is no practical need to build a more enormous, higher tower than the next guy. They strive to reach God deep inside, whether they know it or not. It is part of our inherent evil to reach the heavens and supplant God with ourselves.

Not only do we build towers to the heavens, we now shoot ourselves into outer space under the guise of science and exploration. Although it is fantastic to watch, our efforts are futile. We will not discover alien life; it does not exist. We will not colonize other planets; we can't even run this one. We will not find unknown technologies or resources. The only thing we will accomplish before the Lord's return is the development of new ways to kill one another. This time through weapons, we point at our enemies from outer space. This new pursuit is another way to reach and supplant God with ourselves that comes from deep within our evil desires.

The third item of similarity to the event surrounding Noah's descendants is language. In response to the gathering and the building of the city and tower, God's action was to disperse Noah's descendants and confuse their tongues. Our action is now to reverse God's decision and give ourselves the ability to once again communicate with one another in real-time independent of our local language. New technologies have even given us the ability to accomplish this through holographic projection to put ourselves anywhere in the world.

God said disperse; we say gather. God said no towers; we build towers. God confused our language; we unconfuse our language. Does anyone else see the pattern here, or is it just me? We are a rebellious and sinful lot singularly focused on reversing what God says, putting ourselves on the throne and removing God. Of course, as the scriptures teach and decree, it will not go well for the world at large. The Puppets orchestrating the reversal of God's decrees are beholden to Satan and his plans, setting God to the sidelines. No surprise there.

The big question is how do the Puppets get an unsuspecting, unsupportive, or dissenting world population to give up their national identities, civil liberties, religious freedoms and set aside their local constitutions for this new globalist agenda? The question has been clearly answered over the past couple of years; through fear, intimidation, and the rampant overreach of granted authority.

The Puppets tell us we will imminently meet our doom by a multitude of different events as outlined in the book's opening if they and we do not make an immediate change to the way we do things. Of course, they have the solutions to each catastrophic event outlined. We must comply, capitulate, and adhere to their demands of change and sheepily bow down to the authoritarian rule they have selflessly adopted for our own good. Thank goodness for our saviours - a little sarcasm there.

Unfortunately, they will save nothing and effect no change on the course and direction God has set. God's divine plan and direction mankind, and this planet will take, will in no way be altered or changed by puffed-up men scheming and conniving to usurp power and control over God and the unsuspecting people of this Earth. The only thing they will accomplish is the usurping of our freedoms, replacing them with authoritarian rule and the suppression of our liberties. As stated earlier, we are marching to the end of days on God's terms, and they have no say in the matter.

They will save nothing. You will lose everything to their scheming. Can you reverse their course?

No, unfortunately, you cannot. God describes what the state this world will be in before his return. Like the Puppets, you do not have a say in the matter either. There is nothing you can do to change the course of where we are heading. So what can you do, if anything? Should you become an activist? Should you be trying to save the whales, so to speak? Should you be seeking to topple governments and return control to the people? No, and no to all of the above, as your efforts will be in vain. You will not change God's prophetic vision given to the prophets. It will come to pass.

The first thing is to understand that the fearmongering coming at you from all directions is just that, fearmongering to usurp power. Are there issues with the environment, the weather, the natural disasters, the threat of famine, pestilence, plague, and the list goes on? Yes, there certainly are. These events are described as birthing pains in the last days and the signs of the imminent return of

Christ. You are not going to forestall or change them.

What you can do is know they are coming and prepare for them and the Lord's imminent return. Set aside worry and capitulation to evil authoritarianism and place your trust and faith in your creator and the only one who is in control, God almighty. We will cover what Biblical preparation should look like in a subsequent chapter as laid out in the Bible.

(Matthew 24:3-8)
"As Jesus was sitting on the Mount of Olives, the disciples came to him privately. "Tell us," they said, "when will this happen, and what will be the sign of your coming and of the end of the age?" Jesus answered: "Watch out that no one deceives you. For many will come in my name, claiming, 'I am the Messiah,' and will deceive many. You will hear of wars and rumors of wars, but see to it that you are not alarmed. Such things must happen, but the end is still to come. Nation will rise against nation, and kingdom against kingdom. There will be famines and earthquakes in various places. All these are the beginning of birth pains."

The Puppets purport man has created the issues. We are told our activities on Earth, which they will save us from, are why we are in trouble. The problems have nothing to do with us. The scriptures clearly teach us that they are from God and are great signs from heaven to alert us to the season of the Lord's return. Pretending otherwise is folly and listening to the Puppet's contrived narratives is foolishness.

Don't be duped by their blasphemies and lies. In the next couple of chapters, we will examine some of the lies spewed and bring to light some of the deceptions perpetrated on us. We will expose the truth of the matter at hand. The attempt of the few to suppress and control the many will be revealed. These evildoers enrich themselves and their buddies, who support their scheming at the expense of you and me. Their futile attempt at saving a disposable planet in a constant state of worsening decay is both funny and sad at the same time. Chuckle along with me, as we will now look at their pointless agendas and marvel at their monumental hypocrisies.

GLOBAL WARMING

One of the hot topics of the day is global warming. You can't turn on the TV, radio, or social media channels without being bombarded with the Puppet's doom and gloom message of annihilation by climate change and warming. It is on every news station, both liberal and conservative, and dominates the conversation around the world, not only in your office, home, or local community. They tell us that if we do not make an immediate adjustment to the way we live, the resources we consume, the emissions we generate, and the kicker, control the population growth, it is game over.

The first question is, is this the actual case? Is our planet warming to a level of being life-threatening? It is a little comical that you can find a vast number more accredited scientists speaking out against climate change and global warming than those who support it. This is eyebrow-raising point one. Especially considering the social media giants are censoring and cancelling anyone with an alternative, scientifically-backed viewpoint. You are finished communicating if you question the narrative; your voice is silenced. It does not matter who you are.

Free speech and freedom of expression have been replaced with censorship and ostracization.

I am writing this book in the second half of the year 2021. Right now, I am sitting here in Canada in the dead of winter in -38 degree weather. Oh my, where is this global warming when I really need it? As a matter of fact, there have been record-breaking cold snaps throughout Canada and the US in 2021, along with many other countries. It has not been unique to North America or 2021. Here are just a couple of the headlines.

https://en.wikipedia.org/wiki/February_2021_Nor th_American_cold_wave
On February 7, 2021 Uranium City, Saskatchewan, equaled their all time coldest temperature of −48.9 °C (−56.0 °F) previously recorded on January 15, 1974.

https://bc.ctvnews.ca/21-more-minimum-temperature-records-broken-across-b-c-amid-weather-warnings-1.5721141
BC weather: 42 temperature records broken in 2 days - 3 days ago — More temperature records

were broken in B.C. Monday as most of the province ... More records shattered by cold temperatures ... 25, 2021.

The South Pole just had its most severe cold season on recordhttps://www.washingtonpost.com › weather › 2021/10/01
Oct 2, 2021 — The Amundsen–Scott South Pole Station experienced the coldest average temperature for April to September in 2021 on record.

Antarctica's last 6 months were the coldest on record - CNNhttps://www.cnn.com › 2021/10/09 › weather › weather-r...
Oct 9, 2021 — On February 6, 2020, the Esperanza Research Station recorded a high temperature of 18.3°C degrees (64.9°F). This broke the previous record for ..

I could fill a 1000-page appendix with just recent articles on extreme weather events. The correct narrative is "Extreme Weather Events," as described in the scriptures at the end of days, not global warming as the Puppets tell you. You can do an internet search with your favourite browser to see event after event for the past number of years that have been breaking records on both sides of the ledger – Hot and cold. The actual current history of weather events makes it awfully tough for any critical thinker to be duped by this phoney narrative. It is laughable.

What is it exactly that we are being told is the danger by the Global elites? Ok, sit down; this is devastating. We are told that the Earth will warm by about 2 degrees Celsius by 2050. Or, as of the writing of this book, over the next 29 years on our current course. Yikes, what are we going to do? Oh my goodness, we are all doomed. (A tad more sarcasm) Although this is devastating, our saviours are going to swoop in and save us all. The Puppets have taken immediate action to intervene on our behalf. Like good parents, they have gathered to scold our behaviours and set the ship right by committing to place severe limits on and restrict our activities worldwide.

In what has to be the most hypocritical gathering known to man, the Puppets all gathered in

Glasgow, Scotland, from October 31, 2021, to November 13th, 2021. A staggering 14 days. The gathering was for the event known as the "2021 United Nations Climate Change Conference," better known as COP26, with the 26 standing for the 26th time this conference has been held. The hypocrisy is astounding, with a reported 670 private jets flying world leaders, billionaires, and VIPs to and from the event over the two weeks, creating more carbon emissions in the two weeks than some smaller countries do in a year.

Over 40,000 participants attended this event representing close to 200 countries; a truly international affair: over 22,000 political attendees, 14,000 others, and almost 4000 media personnel. In the group of "Others," you had phoney Scientists, Activists, Billionaires, CEOs, Bankers and a whole host of other "Interested" parties. You had Politicians flanked by entourages of vehicles, staff and security. The billionaires had along with them their aids, families and groupies. The media was accompanied by full crews covering all aspects of production. It was a real superspreader of corruption and greed. Really rather astounding when you consider the positive reporting on the event by the beholden social media and news companies. What a surprise, and talk about irony to its fullest. The folks running and ruining the planet are going to fix it. Maybe a couple more billionaires can take joy rides to space to get a bird eye view of the problems.

Lucky for us, the Puppets were able to develop a plan of action to save the planet. How fortunate are we? They all agreed to uphold the "Paris Climate Accord" agreement hammered out over two weeks in Paris during the United Nations Framework Convention on Climate Change's (UNFCCC) 21st Conference of the Parties (COP 21) and adopted and signed by 196 countries on December 12, 2015. In this accord, the signatories agreed to reduce global warming by half a degree Celsius over the next 29 years from the writing of this book.

Yes, you read that correctly. The imminent threat to life on this planet is a half a degree Celsius increase in temperature over the next 29 years. Who would have guessed? The Puppets have estimated that between now, the writing of this book in 2021, and 2050, the planet will warm by an average of about 2 degrees Celsius. In their infinite wisdom and ~~self-sacrifice~~ with your sacrifices, the goal of achieving warming of only 1.5 degrees Celsius instead of 2 degrees Celsius can be achieved. Well, that is just great news.

(Psalm 2:1-4)
"Why do the nations conspire and the peoples plot in vain? The kings of the Earth rise up and the rulers band together against the Lord and against his anointed, saying, "Let us break their chains and throw off their shackles." The One enthroned in heaven laughs; the Lord scoffs at them."

The first order of business at the conference was to recognize the ~~contrived~~ urgency of the challenge of climate change we are all facing. The conference attendees all agreed that man has contributed to 1.1 degrees Celsius of global warming so far over an undisclosed period of time. I would love to see that math confirmed by proof. Ministers and government bureaucrats from all over the world agreed that countries should come back next year, instead of 2025, to submit stronger emissions reduction targets with the aim of closing the gap to limit global warming to 1.5 degrees Celsius by 2030 rather than 2050. Now I feel better. Maybe they can make it an annual ~~vacation~~ event. Why wait until 2025 to further strip us of our civil liberties and our way of life. Good for them. Three cheers for our saviours, our white knights of hypocrisy.

In addition to accelerating the timeline to reach net-zero emissions by 2050, a new country tracking system would be implemented to measure a countries engagement and commitment to the initiatives outlined at the conference. Yes, again, you heard this correctly, net-zero emissions – none. Can you imagine what an industrialized world looks like that creates no greenhouse gas emissions whatsoever? Back to tents and cooking fires for you. Oh, wait a minute. Cooking on a fire creates emissions. I am sure we can become accustomed to raw food. This new reporting system called the "Nationally Determined Contributions" Synthesis report or NDC will gauge the country's present level of ambition or effort to emissions reduction.

If not for the fact we know this growing hypocrisy is real, and we can physically watch it transforming before our eyes, one would think you were watching a good comedy skit on SNL. The next piece of business on the COP26 agenda was to determine all coal and fossil fuel production and use need to cease. Attendees agreed to a provision calling for a phase-down of coal power and a phase-out of "inefficient" fossil fuel subsidies with an ultimate goal of a reduction to zero extraction and use. Take a second to ponder this initiative and the consequences to your daily living.

The next piece of business was to call out laggards, developed countries with cash, who were not supporting countries that were unable or unwilling to work towards the emission reductions. Developed countries came to Glasgow falling short on their promise to deliver US$100 billion a year for developing countries. Voicing "regret," the Glasgow outcome reaffirms the financial pledge and urges doubling the US$100 billion to US$200 billion. Developed countries expressed confidence that the target would be met in 2023. I can paraphrase that. You will be paying for these initiatives for other countries through your tax dollars. Thank you for taking one for the team.

The COP26 attendees went on dribbling about
this and that throughout the two weeks of the
conference. Ultimately they agreed on the above
items as a collective whole in addition to
completing the items from the COP21 Parris
accords. The COP21 included the implementation
of carbon markets, which will allow countries
struggling to meet their emissions targets to
purchase emissions reductions from other nations
that have already exceeded their targets. This
basically says that the countries that do not comply,
those that are less wealthy than the industrialized
countries, can buy their way out of their agreed-to
responsibilities using the cash supplied to them by
the rich countries. Can you see the hypocrisy here
yet? The whole thing is a joke on us.

As for my family and me, we will trust in and
serve the Lord. We will trust in him to set this
crooked path straight very soon. Woe to those who
do not trust in God. Woe to those who place their
own plans above the plans of the Lord. Vindication
will arrive with a vengeance. Woe to these
deceivers, these unsuspecting Puppets of the Devil.

Our best defence against the hypocrisy is to pray for these lost souls who wander in despair with no real hope, grasping at straws for what they do not understand.

(Psalm 37:1-13)

"Do not fret because of those who are evil or be envious of those who do wrong; for like the grass they will soon wither, like green plants they will soon die away. Trust in the Lord and do good; dwell in the land and enjoy safe pasture. Take delight in the Lord, and he will give you the desires of your heart. Commit your way to the Lord; trust in him and he will do this: He will make your righteous reward shine like the dawn, your vindication like the noonday sun. Be still before the Lord and wait patiently for him; do not fret when people succeed in their ways, when they carry out their wicked schemes. Refrain from anger and turn from wrath; do not fret—it leads only to evil. For those who are evil will be destroyed, but those who hope in the Lord will inherit the land. A little while, and the wicked will be no more; though you look for them, they will not be found. But the meek will inherit the land and enjoy peace and prosperity. The wicked plot against the righteous and gnash their teeth at them; but the Lord laughs at the wicked, for he knows their day is coming."

What we are actually experiencing, in addition to the approach of the end of days for God-directed reasons, is the natural cyclical event of weather. Over 90% of the articles I have researched on weather cycles promote a natural cycle of events with ebbs and flows over time. Considering the Earth is approaching 6000 years in age, yes, 6000 years, not billions or trillions according to the creation story of Genesis and the Biblical narrative. I cover this topic in my upcoming book. We do not have very many years of actual thermometer recorded history. The first continuous record began in England around 1850.

In the absence of historical data, we analyze tree ring growth and width over time, isotope variations in ice cores from the glaciers, borehole temperature analysis, sediment in all environments and geographic locations, and a whole host of other pieces of evidence to determine historical weather patterns. In all circumstances, our efforts of analysis point to the cyclical pattern of warming and cooling of the Earth over time. It is apparent these natural cycles occur over a multitude of time scales, including years, decades, centuries and millennials. We have had periods of severe warming known as interglacial warming and periods of severe cooling known as glacial cooling. There is nothing new or unique about changing weather patterns.

Although we are really not that bright, except in our own minds, we have figured out a couple of things that affect our climate over time. We know that the Earth's orbit around the sun is one of the directors of our weather patterns. These orbital cycles have occurred at different intensities on multi-century time scales. The orbital changes occur slowly over time, influencing where solar radiation is received on the Earth's surface during different seasons. These changes in the distribution of solar radiation are not strong enough to cause significant temperature changes. However, they can amplify the slight warming or cooling effect caused by the orbital cycles.

We also know that ocean-atmosphere interactions regularly cause climate cycles. One of the most well-known cycles is the El Niño which you have probably heard about. It is an interaction between ocean temperatures and atmospheric patterns. These events occur every 3 to 7 years and bring different weather conditions to different parts of the world. Many other cyclical changes occur due to oceanic, atmospheric processes, including the Pacific Decadal Oscillation, which occurs in 25-45 year cycles, and the Atlantic Multi-decadal Oscillation, occurring on approximately 65-85 year cycles.

The moon affects the weather in several indirect ways as well. The moon has a significant effect on ocean tides, and tides have a considerable impact on the temperature in the sense that a world without a moon would experience little or no tides and would have a different system of weather altogether. The moon also affects polar temperatures. Since the moon's gravitational force depends on distance, at any given time, the portion of the Earth closest to the moon is strongly influenced by gravity. This means that when the moon is over an ocean, the water is pulled toward it, creating a tidal bulge. As the moon orbits the Earth, the tidal bulge acts like a wave sweeping around the Earth. This effect causes tides. We know that tides directly impact the conditions described in the above couple of paragraphs.

We know that the fossil record confirms that the planet has gone through intense warming and cooling periods. These cycles began long before we started cutting down trees, driving cars, using hair spray, and allowing idiots to create false narratives. We are talking about complete ecosystem upheaval and change, not half a degree Celsius. Coal, saltwater fish fossils, and sedimented trees have been found in abundance under the ice of Antarctica. Coal is formed in warm tropical areas of vegetation showing the poles were once tropical. Trees don't grow in ice, nor do fish swim in ice, supporting a tropical environment at one point in addition to the flood narrative of scripture.

The fossil record also supports periods of extreme cold with what we call "Ice Ages" that extend from the poles depositing escarpments of collected debris where the ice discontinues its advance. One period of ice advancement extended from the North Pole to southern Ontario, dragging its accumulated debris onto what is now called the

Hamilton Escarpment before retreating back to the pole. The fossil records support five major cold events throughout history that we know of, proceeded by five significant warming events. Let's ignore this actual science and focus on half a degree change over 29 years. Chuckle.

Contrary to what the authoritarians of the day are preaching, this planet will continue on just fine under God's management of his creation. God has created this Earth for us to inhabit until he deems otherwise. We are not going anywhere yet, nor is the planet. Over 1400 references in the scriptures describe God controlling the weather and climate. God has established physical laws by controlling His forces of nature by His divine providence, Word, and power. Godless men will continually look for an alternative narrative to support their evil scheming and deny God as the creator of the heavens and the Earth and all that is in them. God has not been fooled, nor should we be.

(Jeremiah 10:13)
"When he thunders, the waters in the heavens roar; he makes clouds rise from the ends of the earth. He sends

lightning with the rain and brings out the wind from his storehouses."

(Psalm 147:8; 148:8)
"He covers the sky with clouds; he supplies the earth with rain and makes grass grow on the hills."

"lightning and hail, snow and clouds, stormy winds that do his bidding,"

(Job 37: 3, 6, 10-13)
"He unleashes his lightning beneath the whole heaven and sends it to the ends of the earth."

"He says to the snow, 'Fall on the earth,' and to the rain shower, 'Be a mighty downpour.'"

"The breath of God produces ice, and the broad waters become frozen. He loads the clouds with moisture; he scatters his lightning through them. At his direction they swirl around over the face of the whole earth to do whatever he commands them. He brings the clouds to punish people, or to water his earth and show his love."

Have we made mistakes? Sure we have. Have we been bad stewards? Sure we have. We are a fallen, sinful race, with most of our days consumed with ourselves. No wonder we need a saviour. Is the planet going through a slight warming cycle? It appears so with you having no say in the matter. Is the current warming cycle our doom? Nope, our destruction, or better yet, the end of this age as we know it, will come through the events of the book of Revelation as prophecied, and very soon. The Puppets attempt to save a disposable planet destined for destruction and its end by fire on God's timeline. They will save nothing. Maybe they should save themselves by coming to know Jesus Christ as their saviour and repent of their foolishness.

In the following couple of chapters, we will look at what this foolishness will cost you and me in the way of freedoms, lifestyle, and civil and religious liberties.

WHERE'S MY CAR?

Let's take a look at some of what you will be required to give up to achieve the lofty globalist goals of the Puppets, starting with your car, motorcycle, or truck. A mandate to replace all combustion engines with electric vehicles by the year 2035 in industrialized nations is set with the year 2040 for the developing countries.

(Psalm 36:4)
Even on their beds they plot evil; they commit themselves to a sinful course and do not reject what is wrong.

If you happen to drive a car with a combustion engine, one that runs on gasoline or diesel, prepare to give that car up. According to the global elites, you are an evil polluter and part of the problem. Between COP21 and COP26, it has been determined that C02 emissions from carbon and fossil fuels are one of the main culprits of this ~~supposed~~ life-threatening climate change.

Over 30 countries, six major vehicle manufacturers and other actors, like cities, have determined that all new car and van sales will be zero-emission vehicles by 2040 globally and 2035 in leading markets, accelerating the decarbonization of road transportation. Electric cars, or maybe bicycles, here we come. Good luck with implementing the worldwide infrastructure to accomplish this one.

Let's put this goal into a bit of perspective. Currently, statistics show a general estimation of about 1.42 billion operational cars worldwide, including 1.06 billion passenger cars and 363 million commercial vehicles. If we assume an annual production from one electric car plant of 240,000 units a year, the current Tesla production, you would need close to 600 manufacturing plants creating electric vehicles running tomorrow to meet the replacement needs in the next ten years. Well, that's not going to happen.

At the ten-year point, rinse and repeat because the cars produced today will be at the end of their lifecycle ten years from now. The battery cells would never be made in this mass quantity, and I estimate it would take over 50 years to implement the infrastructure to fuel this vast quantity of vehicles electrically.

What does the infrastructure need to look like? The first requirement is the charging stations. Today's electric cars get about 200 miles or 320 kilometres per charge. It is estimated there are about 65 million miles of road globally. If we assume a charging station will be required every 100 miles, there will need to be 650 thousand charging stations built in the next ten years to meet what would be the current charging demand. Are you starting to see how ridiculous this whole exercise of futility is? In addition to this, you will need to pay for and install charging stations at your home and all places of work will need them.

The charging station demand assumes all the road infrastructure is within reach of the electrical grid for the actual power. There is no consideration for those who live in remote areas like myself or others. I live about one hour away from the closest small town with services with no electrical grid between here and there. In actuality, most of the road infrastructure, except for urbanized areas, is not connected to the electrical grid. You can't even get a cellphone signal in most of these more remote areas or connections between larger cities.

Many studies have determined that the production of battery cells and the infrastructure to fuel and implement them are far worse than the emissions of the combined combustion engines worldwide. The extraction and production of lithium alone, the leading component in electric car batteries, has proven to be a nightmare at current levels. Can you imagine when this production is ramped up to meet the replacement of every gasoline and diesel engine on the planet? And don't forget, your smartphone and tablet are also run on lithium batteries.

Lithium is a highly reactive alkali metal with excellent heat and electrical conductivity; the reason it is used for batteries and other items. The current requirement to produce a lithium battery for an automobile is about ten kilograms. 10.6 million metric tonnes of lithium would be required to replace the 1.06 billion cars and trucks with electric vehicles currently in the world.

Here is the kicker. The current estimate of the number of lithium reserves globally is 80 million metric tonnes; it is a finite supply. The total world production of lithium in 2020 was about 82 thousand metric tonnes. How one supposes they will increase the annual supply from 82 thousand tonnes to 10.6 million tonnes is ludicrous.

There are some problems here. The first one is that the lithium supply will run out quickly. Lithium is also used for cell phone batteries, laptops, rechargeable batteries, portable electronics, solar system batteries, ceramics, medicine, medical devices, glass, chemicals, and more. It is estimated that the total annual proposed consumption of lithium will deplete the reserves in 10 years. Now, keep in mind the second problem is we will never produce the projected annual consumption or even come close, so the estimates mean nothing. This is simply another nail in the proverbial coffin of the Puppets scheming. The deeper we look at how ridiculous this whole thing is and apply a little logic to the Puppets plans they fall apart fast.

Another item these ding dongs did not address is their intentions for all of the other forms of travel that require fossil fuel. When they eliminate all fossil fuels, I wonder how they plan to address motorcycles that are not in the above vehicle estimates. It is estimated there are over 200 million motorcycles in the world. There is no current viable electric motorcycle replacement unless you plan to trade your Harley in for an electric Moped. Don't forget airplanes, trains, cruise ships, container ships, industrial machinery, generators, oil furnaces in homes, factory heat, and the list goes on and on.

What about all the secondary or bi-products of petroleum, items we use to run our equipment and lives. Where is the consideration for lubricants, grease, plastics, and so forth? Electronics, textiles, sporting goods, health and beauty products, medical equipment and supplies are full of petroleum by-products. Your household is filled with petroleum by-products from construction materials, shingles, and housing insulation. Add linoleum flooring, glass, furniture, appliances and home decors such as pillows, curtains, rugs, and house paint.

Even many everyday kitchen items, including dishes, cups, non-stick pans, and dish detergent, use oil in their creation. I could fill this entire book with lists of petroleum by-products we rely on daily. There are no words for the level of stupid displayed by these hypocrites who do not have a clue about what they are doing or proposing.

There are a couple of extraction methods for lithium. The lithium water extraction method uses about 500,000 gallons per tonne of lithium. Most of the world's lithium is extracted from a mineral-rich brine around ten metres beneath the briny lakes of high-altitude salt flats. The process of extracting lithium from underneath these salt flats begins by drilling down about 10 meters through the crust and then pumping the brine up to the surface into evaporation pools using water. Once it has gone through an initial evaporation, it is then ready for the next step.

The initial evaporation process creates a salty mud comprised of a mixture of manganese, potassium, borax and lithium salts, which are then moved to another open-air evaporation pool to condense further. The total evaporation time for the brine ranges between 12 and 18 months. Sometimes it sits for years. Once the mud mixture is ready, it is distilled to extract the lithium carbonate, the raw material used in lithium-ion batteries.

The water extraction method is mainly used in Bolivia, Chile and Argentina, known as the lithium triangle. Sixty-five percent of the known lithium reserves, or about 47 million tonnes, are projected to be available in this triangular region. Considering there is little water on or under salt flats where lithium is extracted, and most of the supply is found in impoverished third-world counties, the whole process becomes burdensome on the country's ecosystem and populations even at current production levels. In Chile's Salar de

Atacama, mining activities consumed 65 percent of the region's water which is in short supply, to begin with.

The second type of lithium extraction is called "Hard Rock Extraction." Lithium is extracted from five main types of rocks: spodumene, lepidolite, petalite, amblygonite, and eucryptite. Spodumene is by far the most prominent of the five. Although it yields more per tonne of rock than brine, hard rock mining is about twice as expensive to extract the lithium as described in the brine process above. There are currently about 20 metric tonnes of lithium extracted annually through this process.

The rock extraction process begins with collecting and moving vast amounts of rocks, which are then heated and pulverized. The crushed mineral powder is then combined with chemical reactants, such as sulfuric acid. The slurry is heated, filtered, and concentrated through evaporation and electrochemical processes to form commercial lithium carbonate or hydroxide sold to the market. The process is chemically intensive and consumes a vast amount of electricity and chemicals to complete. Massive mines are constructed and dug for this process, disrupting nearby land and eradicating plant life and the area's natural ecosystem. Many accounts of dead animals and ruined farms in the surrounding regions of these mines have been reported as the farmland is ravaged and mounds of earth moved.

In May 2016, hundreds of protestors threw dead fish onto the streets of Tagong, a town on the eastern edge of the Tibetan plateau. They had plucked them from the waters of the Liqi river, where a toxic chemical leak from the Ganzizhou Rongda Lithium mine had wreaked havoc with the local ecosystem. This was the third such event at this mine. Elsewhere in South America, Argentinians in the Salar de Hombre Muerto natural salt pan have expressed concerns over the lithium mining in the region, citing contamination to streams and the irrigation of crops.

All forms of lithium production are very labour intensive and resource exhaustive, including the precious resource of water that is in short supply where lithium is extracted with water as described above. The social and environmental impacts will continue to degrade as demand, and ultimate production is ramped up. There has also been no consideration for recycling and reclamation of used battery cells as they come to the end of their lifecycle. If we use the current estimation of replacing all combustion engines with electric engines, 1.06 billion used battery cells will be disposed of every ten years. I would imagine the next landfill crisis coming will be the disposal of these spent battery cells, something I am well versed in, considering I spent 22 years in the waste and recycling industry.

The next major issue with setting a mandate to eliminate the use of fossil fuels and carbon or coal in favour of green alternatives is the host of bad actors out there. Who would ever suppose countries like North Korea, Russia, China, Iran, the list is exhaustive, will ever comply with these mandates. When you consider the economy of Russia overall, oil and gas provided 39 percent of the federal budget revenue and made up about 63 percent of Russian exports in 2019. These numbers are much higher today, estimated to be around 73 percent, due to the Biden administration's approval of the Nord Stream 2 pipeline, which Russia will use to carry upwards of 55 billion cubic meters of natural gas to Europe every year. Funny how Russia abstained from attending the COP26.

So, on the one hand, the Puppets are telling us we will no longer have the right to fossil fuels and, on the other hand approving mechanisms to move fossil fuels around the world outside of North America. Does anything look and sound a little fishy here to you, or is it just me? To add to this hypocrisy, due to extreme pressure from the left, the Biden administration cancelled the Keystone XL Pipeline on the first day of office designed to move Canadian oil sands fuel to processers in Canada and the United States.

(Psalm 10:2-4)
In arrogance the wicked hotly pursue the poor; let them be caught in the schemes that they have devised. For the wicked boasts of the desires of his soul, and the one greedy for gain curses and renounces the Lord. In the pride of his face the wicked does not seek him; all his thoughts are, "There is no God." (ESV)

Setting Russia aside to look at some of the oil-producing countries like Saudi Arabia, Kuwait, The United Arab Emirates, and a whole host of others, who supposes that even one of these countries has any intention of abandoning their primary source of revenue anytime soon? In Saudi Arabia in 2020, for example, the petroleum sector accounts for roughly 87 percent of the Saudi budget revenues, 90 percent of export earnings, and 42% of GDP. The Puppets scheme to pull the wool over our eyes and deprive us of our lifestyles for the sole purpose of greed and personal gain. Their scheming under the guise of saving the world is laughable. They are evil men plotting and fulfilling their evil plans at your expense.

There is a prophecy in Ezekiel 38 that describes a cabal of nations coming against Israel in the end days. This horde is led by Gog, the leader of Magog, known today as Russia. Persia, known today as Iran, will partner with Russia and a host of other regional neighbours to come against Israel. This act of war aims to attack Israel to plunder her resources. Up to a couple of years ago, this prophecy was hard to imagine coming to fruition. What would these nations plunder? Maybe some olive oil and a couple of vegetables?

(Ezekiel 38:10-12)
"Thus says the Lord God: On that day, thoughts will come into your mind, and you will devise an evil scheme and say, 'I will go up against the land of unwalled villages. I will fall upon the quiet people who dwell securely, all of them dwelling without walls, and having no bars or gates,' to seize spoil and carry off plunder, to turn your hand against the waste places that are now inhabited, and the people who were gathered from the nations, who have acquired livestock and goods, who dwell at the center of the earth." (ESV)

Low and behold, guess what Israel has discovered. Yes, oil and an abundance of natural gas. What do you suppose Israel plans to do with this newfound wealth of reserves. Yes, pump it into the same markets Russia is courting for their petroleum and natural gas. Well, there is the motive for this prophecy which was not pre-existent before a couple of years ago. Russia will not stand for the Israelis usurping their end markets for their petroleum and natural gas revenues, considering most of their country runs off these revenues. The scriptures also predict this newfound windfall.

(Deuteronomy 33:24-25)
"About Asher he said: "Most blessed of sons is Asher; let him be favored by his brothers, and let him bathe his feet in oil.""

Funny enough as well, in the past couple of years, Russia has made friends with Iran, their regional neighbours, and supports Iran in their nuclear pursuits. Coincidence or the beginning of the fulfilment of prophecy? With how the nations are aligning according to scriptures and how the pieces are falling into place, the Ezekiel War is imminent. Petroleum and fossil fuels are not going anywhere anytime soon, no matter what the evil Puppets are planning and telling you. God's prophecies will be fulfilled in His time and as He directs. A bunch of puffed-up self-serving, god-hating hypocrites who place themselves and their plans above God's are not going to change that fact or hamper God's divine will.

The purpose of this chapter is not to rant about electric vehicles, lithium batteries, or their viability. I believe they are a great thing, and in their time and place, they would ultimately take the natural course of replacing fossil fuels if we were around long enough to see it. We won't be. Jesus is returning for His church imminently. The seven-year tribulation is on the doorstep, which ushers in the end of the church age.

I am endeavouring to point out and prove through common sense and physical practicality the time and place for the Puppets plans is not today and cannot or will not be forced upon us. It is an impossibility. It cannot be achieved in the timeframe being proposed.

No matter how many scare tactics are employed, how many lies and deceptions are perpetrated on the masses, or what evil scheming and plotting the Puppets perpetuate, this planet is not on its way to its imminent demise from contrived global warming. The Puppets perpetuate the lies to forward their globalist agendas and ultimately transfer the control of the world and its direction to them. God has other plans.

What should the Christian's role in all this be? Pray and pray without ceasing. Pray for these lost souls and pray that God's will be done. Know that the church age is drawing to a close and know from where the real struggle comes. These Puppets are unwitting tools of Satan and his minions. He has them by the nose leading them around like sheep to the slaughter doing his will and bidding. I feel sorry for them in their ignorance.

They have no clue they are the Devil's pawns executing his will and purpose. How do we know this? Scripture tells us clearly where our struggles and the world's struggles come from. Our battle is not against man but the Devil. He is the god of this world and uses the unsuspecting to do his bidding. Anyone who does not know God is on the list for him to use as pawns at his will.

(Ephesians 6:10-12)
"Finally, be strong in the Lord and in his mighty power. Put on the full armor of God, so that you can take your stand

against the Devil's schemes. For our struggle is not against flesh and blood, but against the rulers, against the authorities, against the powers of this dark world and against the spiritual forces of evil in the heavenly realms."

(Ephesians 6:18)
"And pray in the Spirit on all occasions with all kinds of prayers and requests. With this in mind, be alert and always keep on praying for all the Lord's people."

Once you are finished praying, prepare for what is coming. In a subsequent chapter, we will get to what Biblical preparation for the Christian should look like.

WHAT ELSE IS COOKING?

At the COP26 conference in Glasgow we looked at above, the comedy show did not end with global warming; you know, reducing the earth's temperature by half a degree Celsius in the next 29 years, as monumental as that was, chuckle. Once they decided they had saved the planet, and good for them, yay, why stop there? They determined that not only would they save the earth from our irresponsible, self-centred, fossil fuel polluting ways, but they would begin to repair the damage that we have done. Isn't that big of them? They are a true vision of inspiration to us lowly serfs who are too stupid to help ourselves.

(Isaiah 1:23)
"Your princes are rebels and companions of thieves. Everyone loves a bribe and runs after gifts. They do not bring justice to the fatherless, and the widow's cause does not come to them."

These altruistic folks broke off into workshops to get to work for the balance of the two weeks of the conference. They broke into separate groups to brainstorm and get to the root of all the world's problems. They worked to devise new and inventive, unattainable, self-serving solutions to all our other perceived planet-wrecking activities. Once again, you were at the center of their focus. Each workshop focused on stripping you of your civil liberties and way of life.

The main goal of these sessions was to devise solutions to curb your activities and your use or consumption of anything they deemed harmful to the planet. They met with the overall agenda and aim of reshaping every sector of the economy at the scale necessary to deliver a net-zero future. Yes, again, you read that correctly; a net-zero future means no greenhouse gas emissions whatsoever of any kind. You had computer guys pretending to be scientists, scientists pretending to be elected political leaders, and political leaders posing as intellects, a real trifecta of stupidity.

(Ecclesiastes 10:1-3)
"As dead flies give perfume a bad smell, so a little folly outweighs wisdom and honor. The heart of the wise inclines to the right, but the heart of the fool to the left. Even as fools

The first item on their cancel list was methane. Methane is classified as a fossil fuel because it is generated and formed from the buried remains of plants and animals. I guess the elites are no longer happy classifying it as the clean alternative to petroleum. I am not sure if they left it out of the general mandate of COP26 because they were not aware of this elementary fact, or they just wanted to attack it separately.

Methane emission sources include landfills, oil and natural gas systems, coal mining, fracking, agricultural activities, including flatulence from cows and other livestock and food production. Other sources include the human waste stream, wastewater treatment, stationary and mobile combustion, forest and campfires, wetlands, and industrial processes.

It looks like the Puppets have their work cut out for themselves. That is a lot of sources that generate methane and is nowhere near an exhaustive list. So, how many of these items can they cancel or eliminate? According to them, all of the sources. It just so happens they have a solution for each one. When they state that the goal is to eliminate all fossil fuel use and achieve net-zero emissions, it all has to go. I wonder if anybody has told them that we might not be too willing to return to a living without any motorized transportation, power, or electrical sources.

The answer to landfills has been floated around for a very long time, both inside and outside government. Some smart fellow devised the terms of zero-waste and 100 percent diversion, meaning landfills will no longer be required if achieved. This fellow's name was Daniel Knapp. He coined the phrases subsequently adopted as goals by the governments and private industry in the 1980s. Since then, our annualized global tonnage going into landfills has increased year over year. Only around 9 percent of plastics get recycled, with the balance going to landfills or incinerated. Well, 42 years later, and we are still working on this one, I guess.

Landfills are not complicated animals. To build a landfill, you dig a big hole and line it with geotextile fabric. Once the liner is in, you start filling it up with garbage and, in today's environment, recyclable material. A leach trench is dug around the edge to contain water leakage that is funnelled to a leachate pond. A berm is usually built around the outer perimeter to hide the monstrosity.

The amount of garbage that goes into a landfill is measured by what they call airspace or how many cubic yards of waste you can fit into the hole. Once the hole has been filled up, a cover of soil is placed over the mound. Methane is generated as the organic composition of the garbage decomposes. The methane, in most cases, is released into the air and burnt through pipes inserted into and through the mound of garbage. In some cases, it is collected for fuel. It is estimated that 20 percent of all methane released into the atmosphere is from landfills.

Most of our recycled plastics went by container ship to China to be repurposed into consumer goods for many years. We could not supply the

Chinese with a clean source of recycled plastics; it was contaminated with garbage. Because of this, the Chinese cut off all external supplies several years ago. Not only do lots of plastics hit the landfills today because of this, but they are also accumulating in old shipping and truck containers, abandoned warehouses and farmer's fields. Oops. As mentioned before, I am well versed in these issues as the former COO of one of North America's largest garbage and recycling companies.

In 42 years, the landfill problem has become progressively worse year over year rather than making any headway with the initiative of 100 percent diversion. How does one suppose to eliminate landfills in the next eight or so years when we have missed the mark for over four decades running? Not only have we missed the mark, but we have also gone the wrong way. It is estimated that over 2.5 billion tonnes of garbage and recycling go to landfills each year globally. I am not referring only to North America in these statistics. The misleading North American statistics will show a slight decline in landfill tonnage. This is only due to misrepresentation and the hiding of tonnages off-book.

Is this a case of uninformed ding dongs making irrational decisions without analyzing or even understanding the facts of the matter at hand? It sure sounds that way to me, and these are the ding dongs we put in charge of our affairs. I suppose we will have to accept some methane from landfills. There goes the net-zero emissions goal in the first item we have examined. Oops again. Maybe we will have better luck with the next couple of items.

(Isaiah 10:1)
"Woe to those who make unjust laws, to those who issue oppressive decrees"

Oil and natural gas systems, coal mining, and fracking all contribute to the release of methane. In the above chapter, we looked at one of the primary uses of oil, which is gasoline production for our cars and trucks. We also examined the proposed solution, and I am confident we discounted the practicality of replacing all vehicles with electric ones any time soon. So there is one more failed initiative to achieving net-zero emissions.

We use coal, natural gas and oil to heat our homes in colder climates, with very few exceptions. To replace every oil or gas burning furnace with green energy in the following decades, let alone a couple of years, is not possible or practical. We are talking about a multi-billion-dollar industry that has developed over the last number of centuries.

We do not have the infrastructure or anywhere close to the manufacturing processes and production plants in place to accomplish this. Also, don't forget the competing initiatives to procure green energy materials like deep cell lithium-ion batteries that we looked at earlier.

Add in the elimination of electricity-producing coal plants, portable generators, portable gas heaters, gas cook stoves, gas-run appliances, barbeques, cutting torches, small airplanes, and many more items to the expanding list. The impracticality of eliminating all these items becomes apparent rather quickly. It is not going to happen.

For the second time, we will have to add the removal of all fossil fuels to our list of failed initiatives to achieve net-zero emissions in the proposed timeline. Methane emissions will continue unabated and most likely will continue to increase.

(John 3:19)
"This is the judgment [that is, the cause for indictment, the test by which people are judged, the basis for the sentence]: the Light has come into the world, and people loved the darkness rather than the Light, for their deeds were evil." (AMP)

The Environmental Protection Agency (EPA) in the United States estimates that 39 percent of all methane emissions come from agricultural activities, including as the main culprits, the composting and use of manure and from farting cows and other livestock. A gentler term might be gastroenteric releases, but it still boils down to cows and livestock passing gas. No, that was not a joke. You can't make this stuff up. They attribute the greatest methane release of all the sources in the world to these bloated beasts and their windy ways.

Of course, the culprit to this increasing problem, according to the Puppets, is population growth and the insatiable need of the growing population to consume meat. It is estimated that meat consumption will increase by 70 percent by 2050 due to population growth and food choices. I am sure you can guess where they are going with this one. Enjoy your meat while you still can.

Several proposals are being floated around for the cure, like developing feed that creates less gas in the critters and managing the manure with bio-digestion and methane collection. I am not sure who the poor soul is who will be out in the pastures collecting the cow poop. That sounds like a crappy job to me. Sorry, I could not resist. UNEP Food Systems and Agriculture Advisor James Lomaxalong, along with most of our illustrious leaders, say the world needs to begin by "rethinking our approaches to agricultural cultivation and livestock production." That includes leveraging new technology, shifting towards plant-rich diets and embracing alternative protein sources.

Did you catch that last part? Let me repeat it. The solution includes shifting towards plant-rich diets and embracing alternative protein sources. Bam! There it is. They are coming for your steaks and burgers—no more barbequed ribs for you. What are alternative sources of protein? Get ready for your new diet of soya beans and quinoa sprinkled with some seeds.

After the flood, God added meat to our diets. Once again, the Puppets set God's decrees aside to replace them with their own, placing their authority above Gods. I think I will be sticking with what God has to say in the matter. I am pretty sure when God created the cows, He knew they might have some gas issues. I am also convinced God was not too worried about a bit of cow flatulence and had no concern about it knocking his created earth out of its orbit.

(Genesis 9:1-5)
"And God blessed Noah and his sons and said to them, "Be fruitful and multiply and fill the earth. The fear of you and the dread of you shall be upon every beast of the earth and upon every bird of the heavens, upon everything that

creeps on the ground and all the fish of the sea. Into your hand they are delivered. Every moving thing that lives shall be food for you. And as I gave you the green plants, I give you everything."

Point to the Genesis passage above if anyone tries to tell you that God does not want you eating meat. God decrees, "Every moving thing that lives shall be food for you." This group of elites' arrogance and misguided notions are astounding, to say the least. To watch these globalists place their authority above God's authority is beyond comprehension and belief. One day they will stand before Him to give an accounting. I would shudder to be them on that day of reckoning.

Once again, we will have to add this one to the list of failed initiatives to reduce methane gas emissions. Given the world's food shortage and the increasing population, I am convinced farming and meat production is not going anywhere. They can try, but could you imagine some knob-kneed politician trying to tell a Texas redneck he can't have a steak? That would be fun to watch. So far, the score is 0 for reaching net-zero emissions. As a matter of fact, my calculations have them increasing over time as we travel to God's ultimate return. Are you starting to see the hypocrisy of this whole exercise in futility the Puppets are perpetrating?

Next on the list of methane-producing culprits is the human waste stream and wastewater treatment plants. The only way to curb the piles of feces we generate is to have less of us running around. Low and behold, they have a plan for that as well. You will read estimates of the optimum world population to be anywhere between 500 thousand and 3 billion. That would mean at least 4 billion of us will have to check out to satisfy their estimates.

You hear the term sterilization, either forced, unforced or by secret means. They throw around legislated mandated birth control. They tell us there is the possibility of a vast natural death from some worldwide ~~plandemic~~ pandemic or disease. Possibly war, nuclear war, or maybe famine could get a bunch of us. All you have to do is a cursory internet search to see how rampant this thought process has become. I will not spend more time here covering this topic as I cover it in-depth in my new book released in early 2022, "Tribulation Training."

Know for the purpose of this book that the globalist elites are not happy with the number of us running around. The messaging is coming from every one of our Puppet groups and the world institutions like the United Nations and the World Health Organization. Once again, they choose to play God and are singularly focused on bringing the numbers down, second only to their climate change agendas. God says be fruitful and multiple, as we read earlier in Genesis. The Puppets say stop being fruitful and stop multiplying. Hopefully, you are not on their list for reduction.

And once again, we are going to have to score the goal of net-zero emissions as a failure. Even if there were some possibility that the population could be reduced to say, 3 billion, you would still have 3 billion people creating methane from their bodily function. I predict with certainty that the population will continue to increase and deliver methane into the atmosphere.

Next on the hit list is stationary and mobile combustion, forest or wildfires and campfires. Combustion is defined as incineration or burning of all types. Incineration can include combustion engines to incineration plants that produce electricity by burning all forms of waste. We have already covered combustion engines, so let's look at electricity-producing incineration plants.

There are two choices for waste disposal, landfills and incineration. Is one better than the other as a pollutant? Landfills spew methane into the atmosphere when it is not collected. Very few landfills actually collect methane. Incineration plants emit greenhouse gases into the atmosphere. If you had to choose one, I would select incineration as at least you create the by-product of electricity for consumption. The point here is, no matter which one we look at, they both create emissions and are going nowhere anytime soon. Another fail for the deceivers.

Forest fires have some good as well as the bad and are a renewing force from God. They stimulate new growth, release valuable nutrients from the forest floor, and open sunlight to the canopy. They allow some evergreens to reproduce better, opening their cones and freeing their seeds. Fire removes the low-growing underbrush, cleans the forest floor of debris, opens it up to sunlight, and nourishes the soil reducing the competition for nutrients and sunlight that is an ever-raging battle within the forest.

I am absolutely confident the Puppets have no say in when, where, and how forest fires start. This is beyond even their perceived and self-proclaimed omnipotence. I also know that forest fires will continue as we move into these last of the last days. They will increase in quantity and intensity, which we will look at in a bit. Another fail for the Puppets goal of achieving net-zero emission in the near future.

Campfires, hmm, that's an easy one for them. I am sure they will be coming for your campfire very soon. Better bring your propane stove to cook. Oh, wait, you are losing that too. Ok, bring a baggie of tofu and mung beans for your meals. Enjoy. What is most comical about this one is one severe forest fire anywhere in the world pumps more methane and greenhouse gas emissions into the atmosphere than all the campfires burnt in the world for the last decade. The Puppets can have a win on this one with little to no effect of emission reduction. It was reported last year that the smoke from Canadian wildfires was making its way all the way to Europe, as seen in the article below.

Wildfire smoke makes it to Europe…
https://www.washingtonpost.com › weather › 2020/09/16

Next on the methane hit list is wetlands. It is estimated that natural wetlands produce over 30 percent of the global methane emissions. The water-logged soils in wetlands are the ideal breeding grounds for methane production. It is estimated that between 6 percent and 10 percent of the world's landmasses are wetlands. Wetlands are found in almost every region of the world and are considered the most biologically diverse of all ecosystems. They provide habitat for a significant number of water and land species. Unless the Puppets plan to fill them all in, a task I am sure they are not planning to undertake, wetlands will continue to emit methane at their current levels. This one will be a fail on our net-zero emissions scorecard.

Although we could spend all day looking at sources of greenhouse gas emissions, including methane, both natural and manufactured, we will look at just one more – industrial production. All the consumer goods you use and consume started their lifecycle with raw materials of some type. The raw materials could be plastic polymers, Wood, cotton, metal of all forms, both ferrous and non-ferrous, plant matter, and so on.

Every raw material goes through a process of refinement, combination, and manufacture or assembly to arrive at your doorstep in its completed form. In almost all cases, the method of extraction and refinement produces greenhouse gas emissions, including methane. You have to look no further than any industrial park in any city to see the chimney stacks belching their grunge and pollution into the atmosphere. Once again, our pundits have attached a percentage of 30 percent emission contribution to industrial production.

The world economies, measured by gross domestic product (GDP), are the driving forces of the economic measurement of a countries advance or decline, success or failure. The elites have enriched themselves by manufacturing goods, providing services, and investing in the markets that drive these economies. It is what we call capitalism. It is all about money and always will be. Money, power, and prestige are their gods. These are the things in life they idolize. Your well-being is not at the core of their initiative, nor will it ever be.

It will be a cold day in the bottomless pit before they ever shut these processes down or even limit them for the good of the planet. When it comes to affecting their stock portfolios or personal wealth, the narrative suddenly changes. They follow the mantra, do as I say, not as I do. Man is evil by our fallen nature and wicked to the core. God-hating, Self-serving global elitists, billionaires, politicians, and those enriching themselves will continue to do so at your expense. You will be the ones they require the sacrifices from as they continue in their hypocrisies unabated.

On a side note and of interest, if you follow along with the math percentages of the emission contributions, we are already well over 100 percent and have not attached a score to half of the topics. There is a surprise. The pundits are just pulling numbers out of a hat and have no real clue what they are talking about, or they are just bad at math.

The sole purpose of this chapter has been to show the hypocrisy and outright ludicrous dealings of the Puppets with reality. I am not sure if they think we are all stupid or if the devil's schemes have so blinded them they no longer operate with sound minds and judgement. I am not suggesting we should not be good stewards of this earth or act responsibly towards it; of course, we should. What is in question is who is ultimately in control? God is in complete control and knows how to manage His creation. God does not need these beholden Puppets of the Devil calling the shots or attempting to usurp His control and divine authority.

JUST RIGHT

In our first chapter of the book titled "In The Beginning," we opened with the very first verse of the Bible in the book of Genesis. The verse describes God's creation of this world. In the second verse, God describes the initial state of the world after He created it.

(Genesis 1)
"In the beginning God created the heavens and the Earth. Now the Earth was formless and empty, darkness was over the surface of the deep, and the Spirit of God was hovering over the waters."

I often sit in quiet contemplation over the sheer magnitude, majesty and wonder of God and who He is. Comprehending God's true infinite power and glory escapes me. My mind is too finite, with too many restrictive qualities to fully understand God's might. We often spend our days running to and fro, back and forth, up and down, with little or no thought to the purpose of what we do and why we do it. We just get things done because they are on our list of things to do. Seldom do we take the time to be still and know God, as we are instructed to do. We allow our lives to be all-consuming, leaving little time for our creator.

(Psalm 46:10)
"Be still and know (recognize, understand) that I am God. I will be exalted among the nations! I will be exalted in the earth." (AMP)

When we take the time to consider who God is and His creation, we can be left with nothing but wonder and awe. You can be left with no other conclusion as you look into the heavens that they are a created marvel of splendour with design and purpose. As scripture says, we are left with no other alternative but to know God as the creator. The heavens and the earth declare his glory. We simply need to look up and gasp at what God created for our pleasure and home. Those who choose to scoff at God as the creator are left without an excuse or a defence when gazing up at His creation. It speaks for itself.

(Romans 1:20)
"For ever since the creation of the world His invisible attributes, His eternal power and divine nature, have been

clearly seen, being understood through His workmanship [all His creation, the wonderful things that He has made], so that they [who fail to believe and trust in Him] are without excuse and without defense." (amp)

When you consider the true creative power, imagination, creativity and splendour of God, you are left with nothing but amazement and appreciation. Your desire becomes to exalt Him and praise His name morning, noon, and night. I can no longer imagine a life without knowing God as my creator and that I reside in His creation that he has made and upholds specifically for you and me.

(Isaiah 45:18)
"For thus says the Lord, who created the heavens (he is God!), who formed the earth and made it (he established it; he did not create it empty, he formed it to be inhabited!): "I am the Lord, and there is no other." (ESV)

For those who do not know God, the earth is a terrifying place. No wonder they seek, in their own power, to reverse what they deem threatens their survival and the survival of the planet. No wonder they seek an alternate home on another planet or even in another solar system, believing this one we live on is ultimately doomed. How could they believe otherwise without knowing and trusting in God? These God mockers and scoffers can only rely on their own perceived intellect and abilities to try and save themselves. What a sad commentary and a tragic way to go through life.

When you look at the state of this planet without knowing God is in complete control, you can make no other determination that all life on earth, and the earth itself, has a finite life span and that it will ultimately meet its doom and be destroyed. We have no ability on our own to extend the planet's ability to sustain life or exist as we know it. Basic science tells the story of the earth's ultimate doom. One needs to look no further than the sun or the earth itself for the fundamental truth of these statements.

The sun is no different than a propane tank for your barbeque. Your barbeque tank gets filled with propane, lit, and then the gas is burnt through a grill until it is empty. The sun is just a giant version of a barbeque tank. It is a ball of gases slowly burning itself out. Its fuel source is finite, just like the barbeque propane tank we use to heat our food. It will run out of fuel one day.

When the gases in the sun are consumed or reduced to a level that no longer generates the heat we need to survive, it is game over for the planet and all who are living on it. Or, at least it would be if God were not in control of His creation and upholding and sustaining all things.

(Hebrews 1:3)
"The Son is the radiance and only expression of the glory of [our awesome] God [reflecting God's [a]Shekinah glory, the Light-being, the brilliant light of the divine], and the exact representation and perfect imprint of His [Father's] essence, and upholding and maintaining and propelling all things [the entire physical and spiritual universe] by His powerful word [carrying the universe along to its predetermined goal]. When He [Himself and no other] had [by offering Himself on the cross as a sacrifice for sin] accomplished purification from sins and established our freedom from guilt, He sat down [revealing His completed work] at the right hand of the Majesty on high [revealing His Divine authority]," (AMP)

The scientists of the day will tell you our solar system is somewhere between 10 and 15 billion years old. They tell us that it will be another 6 to 8 billion years before the sun burns itself out and that we should have no immediate concern. Unfortunately, they have no clue about what they espouse as fact, and I have zero confidence in their predictions. According to the Genesis account of creation, our solar system and planet are just under 6,000 years in age.

From the genealogies in scripture, two thousand years have passed from creation or Adam to Abraham. Two thousand years have passed from Abraham to the crucifixion. One thousand nine hundred and ninety years have passed from the crucifixion to the current time. The only way to come up with a different answer, give or take a couple of years, is to discount the truth of the scriptures. By God's account, the genealogies of scripture place our solar system and the earth around five thousand nine hundred and ninety years old. I am sticking with God's math rather than the whimsical tales of today's lost souls claiming what is fiction to be fact.

Even some professing Christians will claim the Genesis account is allegorical and fall into the trap of embracing the flawed scientific models of the age of the earth being billions of years old. They will tell you a day of creation was not really 24 hours but potentially thousands or even millions of years. This is either pure ignorance or a lack of understanding or belief in what the scriptures teach. God said he created the heavens and the earth in six literal days. Full stop and end of the story. To assume anything else of God's recounting or discounting His words is heresy.

No other explanation makes sense. Only God's description of the creation timeline in six days is feasible. As examples. The Hebrew word for day, Yom, as in English, is used both for a literal, twenty-four-hour day and also for an indefinite period of time, such as in the expression "For the day of the Lord is at hand" (Joel 1:15). However, the word Yom always means a twenty-four-hour literal day when used with a numeral, day one, day two, first day, second day, etc. There are no exceptions to this rule. Yom is used with an integer in the Genesis Creation account, indicating that it intends the reader to understand that these are literal days of twenty-four hours.

When the Israelites were wandering in the wilderness, God supplied food known as manna every morning. They were to gather only enough for one day's use. Anything more than that would spoil by the following day. However, they were to gather twice the usual amount of manna on Friday because none would be available on the Sabbath, Saturday morning. When they gathered extra manna on Friday for use on Saturday, the extra manna did not spoil (Exodus 16:11-26). This illustrates that the weekly Sabbath, marking each cycle of seven literal days, continued to be a memorial of Creation week. Thus, the weekly cycle is evidence that the days of creation were literal days of twenty-four hours.

Let's look at the seven-day week next. As a unit of time, the week has no basis in the natural movements of the earth, moon, or the sun, as do the day, the month, and the year. Other than the week of creation described in Genesis, there seems to be no basis for the week as a unit of time. This, too, argues that the Creation week in Genesis was a week of seven literal days.

God set aside the seventh day of Creation week as a holy day of rest. The Israelites kept the Sabbath in the wilderness and continued to observe it in the time of Christ (Luke 4:16; 23:55, 56). We also see this in Acts 17:2. Orthodox Jews continue to keep the seventh-day Sabbath even today. The changes made to the calendar through time have not affected the weekly cycle of seven days. The integrity of the weekly cycle continues and is evidence for the Creation week being composed of seven literal days.

The view that each day of the Genesis Creation account is thousands or millions of years, rather than literal days of twenty-four hours, does not work. Genesis says that plants were created on the third day (Genesis 1:11-13), and sunlight was created on the fourth day (Genesis 1:14-19). If the third day is a long time period of hundreds, thousands or millions of years, how could plants have existed without sunlight? Likewise, many plants require insects for pollination. How could these plants have survived and reproduced without insects that God did not create until the sixth day (Genesis 1:24, 25)?

The fourth commandment (Exodus 20:8-11) links the Sabbath of the seventh day with the weekly cycle of seven days. The word "remember" at the beginning of this commandment would be useless if the 24-hour days were actually hundreds, thousands, or millions of days long. Even days described as 100 years long do not work. Only 24-hour periods for a day can fit the narrative. No one would ever "remember" because they would all be dead! The admonition concerning six days of labour and one day of rest would be meaningless.

In the first two chapters of Genesis, the wording of the creation account can only be understood as meaning literal days. There is no other possible explanation, and it only makes common sense. The expressions used such as "day and night," "evening and morning," "light and darkness" only make sense when applied to a 24-hour period of time. We know the light and dark cycles of the earth exist because we experience them every 24 hours without fail. We attach the terms evening and morning and day and night to these 24-hour cycles just as God did.

The genealogy of Adam begins with his creation on day six. Adams Genealogy counts the generations down by days to the day of Christ and his birth. With the unearthing of the Dead Sea Scrolls coupled with the historical accounts, this genealogy is accurate. One can only conclude that the 6th creation day was a literal 24-hour day. If it was anything more than that, the genealogies are useless, as would the entirety of the scriptures be. You can't have more than 24 hours between day six and Gods rest on day 7 for any of the prophecies to be accurately tied to the timeline of the Biblical history of events and Adams's birth to the birth of Jesus Christ.

Knowing the days of creation were six literal 24 hour periods supports the age of the earth as a young planet as indicated above and by the scriptures. There is no alternative option without discarding the word of God. Sadly, this is what the scientific community does. Praise God for the truth of scripture and the literal sense of its writing. Now back to our discourse on God's infallible and unerring control of His creation.

This sphere we call home, earth, is a ball of molten gasses and rock with a solid inner core and a molten outer core surrounded by a thin crust that we reside on. Estimates put the temperature of the earth's inner core anywhere between 2,000 and 9,000 degrees Celsius and the outer core in the range of 2,000 and 7,000 degrees Celsius. Depending on which scientist or group you read will depend on what estimate you end up with. They have no clue though they, as in most things, pretend they do.

Our earth hurtles through space at a staggering 107,000 kilometres per hour as it travels in its orbit around the sun every 365 days. In addition to this, it makes one complete revolution on its axis every 23 hours, 56 minutes and 4 seconds rotating between 1,600 and 1700 kilometres per hour. The gravity of the sun is constantly pulling the earth towards it. The speed of the planet, and its orbital travel, coupled with centrifugal force and the other gravitational forces from our solar system and planets, keep the earth from either falling into the sun and burning up or flying wildly off into space. It is an intricate, fragile dance of opposing forces that keep us aloft.

If just one thing goes wrong in this highly choreographed pirouette of planets and forces, it is game over. If I did not know God, I would cower for my life daily, assuming the worst and petrified of just one of these forces failing. It is understandable why those who do not know God have this internal need to attempt to mitigate a presupposed risk to the survival of this planet.

The good news is God is the one who created the heavens and the earth and all that is in it. God sustains it all, holds it in place, and ensures nothing will happen to it outside of His divine will with his word and power. There is zero risk of planetary annihilation with God controlling and managing his creation from either inside or outside forces. The planet will continue to rotate on its axis, in its place, just where God put it.

As mentioned earlier, spraying a couple of cans of hairspray, driving our cars, or cutting down some trees is not going to send the planet spinning into oblivion. God is in complete control at all times. He is aware of all that happens in and on His planet. The planet is His; we are temporary visitors. The Puppets have it wrong because they do not know or trust in God.

(Nehemiah 9:6)
"You alone are the Lord. You made the heavens, even the highest heavens, and all their starry host, the earth and all that is on it, the seas and all that is in them. You give life to everything, and the multitudes of heaven worship you."

(Colossians 1:17)
"And He Himself existed and is before all things, and in Him all things hold together. [His is the controlling, cohesive force of the universe]." (AMP)

For our planet to sustain life, God had to get everything just right. We know that he did, or we would not be here. Each planet in our solar system has to follow the exact orbit they are travelling in at the speed they do to sustain their trajectories, avoid collisions or upset the balance of their orbits. If one flies off course, the system collapses. The level of coordination and mathematical precision God uses to accomplish this is beyond comprehension. We have to be at precisely the proper distance from our sun to keep the planet at the correct temperatures to sustain life. To close, and we burn, too far, and we freeze. Good thing God got that just right as well.

Our solar system has to be in exact alignment with all the other heavenly bodies and play its part in God's grand design. If we woke up to find our system was careening towards a collision course with another galaxy, once again, game over. It looks like God got this one correct as well. Not only did he get it right when he placed all the stars and planets in their designated location, but He also went so far as to give each one a name. How cool is that? Our Milky Way Galaxy is just one of billions of galaxies in the universe. There are at least 100 billion stars within it, and on average, each star has at least one planet orbiting it.

No one can conceivably see or count all the galaxies out there. Some estimate that there are over 200 billion trillion stars in the galaxies, not counting the planets that would be evidently there. I am guessing no one really has a clue, and the number is probably far more significant than this. How could one name every one of them is beyond me; however, as God says, it is not beyond him, and He has given each one a name and set it in its place. How is that for an awesome God?

(Isaiah 40:26)
"Lift up your eyes on high And see who has created these stars, The One who leads forth their host by number, He calls them all by name; Because of the greatness of His might and the strength of His power, Not one of them is missing."

In addition to dealing with all of the intricacies of getting the entirety of the solar system just right, God had more work to do. For our continued survival, God had to also design and manage the conditions on and within our planet. The atmosphere needed the precise combination of 78 percent nitrogen and 21 percent oxygen with trace elements of other gases so we could breathe.

The seasons needed to be designed in such a way to support agriculture and livestock rearing—the ecosystem required to be just right to sustain all creatures and plant life. Atmospheric oxygen renewal through filtration was needed to maintain the required balance to sustain life. The gravitational system had to be just right to promote muscle growth as we move around and to keep our feet on the ground.

You get the picture. Only an omnipresent, omnipotent, all-powerful omniscience God could have been up for the task. Chance and evolution? Chuckle, who are you kidding? We have not even considered the complexity of you or me and all the complex systems within our bodies that also had to be just right.

The continuing moral of the story is God knows what he is doing, has gotten things just right, and has things under control. The Puppets run around pretending the sky is falling. They use scare tactics and instill terror into the unsuspecting to drive their agendas and instill their will on you. Their agendas conflict with God's agenda. I am confident God will win the day. We know God maintains this planet, and if He believes it is necessary to clear the atmosphere up, he will do just that with a breath.

We can also have complete confidence in God, not just because he is the creator of all that is, but because he tells us he will maintain this world until He is done with it. He tells us that while this earth remains, that seedtime and harvest, the seasons, summer and winter, the hot and cold temperatures, will remain as well. When God decrees it, I believe it with all my heart, mind, and soul.

I have no right to question God's providence or will. He will renew the ground when it is needed and does not need our help. They, or we, have no say in the matter, and there is nothing we can do that will change this fact. Their narrative of global warming and everything else they are spewing is folly. They are lost souls spreading a false narrative because they know not God.

(Revelation 4:11)

"Worthy are You, our Lord and our God, to receive glory and honor and power; for You created all things, and because of Your will they existed, and were created."

(Genesis 8:22)

"While the earth remains, Seedtime and harvest, And cold and heat, And summer and winter, And day and night Shall not cease."

(Psalm 104:30)

"You send forth Your Spirit, they are created; And You renew the face of the ground."

So sayeth the Lord! Amen!

Although I consider myself a student of science, I am not a scientist. I am a Biblicist, one who believes in the unerring, inspired, infallible Word of the living God and in all that it says and teaches. This belief resides within the framework of believing the Bible has been written literally, allowing for symbolism, imagery, and types. If any theory, instruction or purported fact contradicts in any way the word of God, that theory, instruction or purported fact is false. Seek the truth through the Word and discard all falsehoods contrary to it. Full stop.

NATURAL DISASTERS

As we have looked at in the preceding chapters, the governments, global elites or billionaires, and scientists use the false global warming narrative to scare you into submission. This submission drastically alters and severely restricts your lifestyles and activities.

Your liberties and freedoms are being suppressed, and it will only worsen as we march towards the end of days. Instead of calling out the climate fluctuations for what they are, the natural cycle of warming and cooling, they monger fear to execute their agendas. And, of course, you are the target of this fear.

How is this fear instilled into the populous? We know the tools they use to deliver their message, the beholden media and social media platforms. We also know that one unified message is being delivered around the world. We need to look no further than any news channel. Each one provides the same message, almost verbatim. The bigger question is, how is it nearly the entirety of the world has fallen for their deceptions and false narrative?

Has the world been deceived? Revelation 12:9 helps us with our answer.

(Revelation 12:9)
"And the great dragon was thrown down, the age-old serpent who is called the devil and Satan, he who continually deceives and seduces the entire inhabited world; he was thrown down to the earth, and his angels were thrown down with him." *(AMP)*

Satan is the great deceiver and seducer of the world and of those who are beholden to him. He is the god of this world. Those who have joined his team are deceived and seduced into carrying out his will. Only two teams are running; Gods and Satan's. If you are not on the one, you are on the other. There is no middle ground like some would like to pretend. The end of the verse in Revelation 12:9 also gives us a little further insight into Satan and his team. Not only has he conscripted all those on earth who do not call on God, his followers, angels now known as demons, are also carrying his flag and doing his bidding on this earth as his workers of iniquity.

(2 Corinthians 4:4)

"among them the god of this world [Satan] has blinded the minds of the unbelieving to prevent them from seeing the illuminating light of the gospel of the glory of Christ, who is the image of God."

(Luke 11:23-24)

"Whoever is not with me is against me, and whoever does not gather with me scatters." (ESV)

If the Puppets were only to tell us that the climate would warm by 2 degrees Celsius over the next 29 years and that by taking their prescribed actions, we can reduce the number by one-half a degree Celsius, we would all laugh at them. The circumstance must appear much more dire and life-threatening than a puny half a degree to get our attention and submission. They need to have a compounding problem, and more than one of them, with equal to or more significant perceived risks than their single climate change narrative they are spewing.

Lucky for them, not so fortunate for us, the planet is complying with their needs. There is no better way to stoke and propagate fear than to find additional villains. What better villains can there be than natural disasters? Maybe we can attribute every natural disaster that occurs to climate change. That is precisely what they have decided to do and are doing. It does not matter what type of event occurs; if it is catastrophic, the perceived climate change is blamed. Heck, it does not even need to be a disastrous event anymore. Even regular, natural events that happen all the time are now blamed on the climate.

It is funny how a parrel event that exactly mimics the climate change narrative is taking place as I write this book. This little pandemic is running around right now, infecting the world. Although it has a 99.97 percent survival rate and generally affects the elderly or those with a compromised system or pre-existing condition, they have shut the whole world down. The question to ask is what has happened to the common cold or influenza-the flu. These regular seasonal events that have been with us forever appear to have vanished into thin air.

An informed person with half a brain realizes these other illnesses have not magically disappeared. The Puppets ensure doctors and hospitals classify and attribute pretty well every sickness known to man to this new illness. It is a course in fear-mongering 101. Most illnesses are attributed to the new virus, so are a majority of the deaths. It appears that critical thinking and the application of common sense are characteristics of the past as the majority of the people have fallen hook line and sinker for the lies. It just makes no logical sense. Have we just checked our brains at the door and become pawns of the elites? What is afoot?

Ok, back to our climate narrative. I could not resist poking the bear with the parallel event listed above. Sometimes you just have to have a little fun. Although off-topic, it does help us to recognize a scary pattern that is developing. This new pattern we see developing places blame on something other than where it belongs. Only by miss direction and subterfuge can they successfully pull off their deceptions. The comical events and discourses we are now subject to remind me of two kids getting their hands caught in the cookie jar, each pointing at the other as the culprit.

We can clearly see that natural disasters are on the rise; they are measurable statistics. There are two questions to answer. The first question is, is the spike in natural disaster events normal and actually happening or is something new happening? The second question to consider is the cause of the spike in these events. The Puppets parrot their answer of global warming for everything. The Bible has a contradictory explanation to our supposed experts. Like in all other situations, I will go with the Bible's answer over the lies of these Puppets of Satan who in and of themselves are now great deceivers. They have become quite adept at spinning their lies and deceit.

We do not have to look any further than the day's headlines to answer our first question. If you do an internet search for "are natural disasters increasing due to climate change?" on Google alone, you will find over 89,700,000 pages of news articles and blogs that will answer with a resounding yes. Assuming about ten entries per page, we get almost one billion responses to this single question. There is no surprise there; however, we confirm how hot the topic is today.

Suppose we set the news sites and blogs aside, knowing that most are no longer delivering news but rather unsubstantiated propaganda. In that case, our subsequent enquiry should be to pull out some recorded statistics to find our true answers. Although the news sites do an excellent job reporting the events, they fail to communicate the causes correctly, choosing to write what the Puppets tell them to write.

We will define a natural disaster as forest or wildfires, floods, tsunamis, volcanic eruptions, hurricanes, and earthquakes, just to name a couple. We will assume the result of natural disasters are drought, famine, pestilence, plague, species in distress, shoreline erosion and human death, to name a couple of the results a natural disaster provides. We will consider the cause-and-effect syndrome meaning the one event causes the subsequent event. Let's look at some statistics first.

Naturally occurring wildfires are most frequently caused by lightning. There are also volcanic, meteor, and coal seam fires depending on the circumstance. Wildfires caused by humans range from power lines on trees, discarded cigarette butts, fireworks, campfire mismanagement, arson and a whole host of more reasons. Wildfires are not limited to any particular area and can flare up anywhere in the world. There are two main ways wildfires are measured: the fire's duration and the acres burnt.

A 2017 report by the US Global Change Research Program recorded a "profound increase in forest fire activity" in recent decades. In 2020 there were 58,950 wildfires compared with 50,477 in 2019, according to the National Interagency Fire Center. About 10.1 million acres burned in 2020, compared with 4.7 million acres in 2019.

You will see fluctuations up and down within decades. When you do a decade-over-decade review, there has been a substantial increase in frequency worldwide. It also stands to reason that as the population grows, so will the fires caused by human activity. Wildfire management has also become intricately more advanced over the last number of decades, helping to control the duration of wildfires and, in some areas, the frequency. Most point to global warming as the cause of the increases. I point to God as we will look at the scriptural explanation in a bit for these events.

Are floods and tsunamis an event of the day? In the past 100 years, 58 tsunamis have claimed more than 260,000 lives or an average of 4,600 per disaster - more than any other natural disaster. Tsunamis are caused by earthquakes happening on converging tectonic plate boundaries in the open waters, landslides, volcanic activity, weather, and asteroids or meteors of a sufficient size that breach the earth's atmosphere and land in the ocean.

It is of unanimous consent that tsunamis will grow in frequency and devastation with rising sea levels due to the current melting of the glaciers. They will only get worse, much worse, as time marches on.

How about floods? Floods are the accumulation of excess water over dry land. They are caused by the overflow of inland waters or tidal waters. They can also be caused by an accumulation of water from sources such as heavy rains or dam breaches or breaks. Flooding can be classified into three categories, Coastal flooding, urban flooding, and flash flooding.

Due to the melting icebergs and coastal storm surges, higher sea levels are eroding coastal banks at an alarming rate and will affect over 40% of the total population worldwide. Urban flooding is caused by excess rain or dam breaks overwhelming the local extraction system. You need to look no further than your local news stations to track these never-ending events. Flash floods are quick rising floods caused by excess rainwater or melting ice on frozen ground. All three events continue to increase in frequency and severity year over year drastically. Once again, you need to look no further than the nightly newscast for confirmation. Something is up.

What is an earthquake, and how do they happen? Although the Earth appears solid from our perspective, it's actually extremely active just below the surface. The solid crust and the stiff layer of the mantle we live on make up a region called the lithosphere. The lithosphere isn't a continuous piece that wraps around the whole earth. It's made up of tectonic plates. Tectonic plates are constantly shifting as they drift around on the viscous, or slowly flowing, mantle layer below.

These moving plates cause stress on the Earth's crust. These stresses lead to cracks called faults. When tectonic plates move, it also causes movements at the faults. An earthquake is the sudden movement of the Earth's crust at a fault line. The Richter magnitude scale assigns a number to measure the amount of seismic energy released by an earthquake. It is a base-10 scale. The higher the number, the more intense an earthquake is. Anything over a score of seven is considered severe and can cause significant damage and death.

Each year we experience earthquakes throughout the world. Our records indicate we should expect about 16 major earthquakes in any given year at our current point in time. That includes 15 earthquakes in the magnitude 7 range and one earthquake magnitude 8.0 or greater. Our records show that we have exceeded the average number of significant earthquakes several times in the past number of decades. The trend lines also show the number of earthquakes increasing per year through time, as shown by the chart below as per the National Oceanic and Atmosphere Administration.

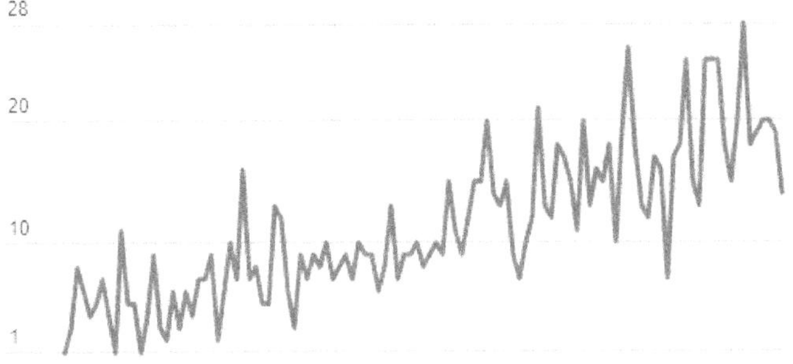

We have seen a 265 percent increase in earthquake activity over the past century,

Like other natural disaster events, we observe fluctuations within decades, but the overall increase in frequency is clearly evident and will continue according to the scriptures.

The last natural disaster event we will look at is volcanoes. A volcano is a rupture in the crust of the Earth that allows hot lava, volcanic ash, and gases to escape from a magma chamber below the surface. We find volcanoes where tectonic plates are diverging or converging. Most volcanoes are found underwater. Considering over 71 percent of the earth is covered by water, this makes sense. Volcanoes can also form where the Earth's plates stretch and move due to conflicting pressures.

Significant eruptions can affect atmospheric temperature as ash and droplets of sulfuric acid obscure the sun and cool the Earth's troposphere. Significant volcanic eruptions can result in volcanic winters. A volcanic winter reduces global temperatures caused by this volcanic ash and droplets of sulfuric acid and water obscuring the Sun for an extended period. We have seen a drop in local temperatures by 2 to 3 degrees lasting 2 to 3 years in recent history.

There are umpteen accounts of the weather being affected after a significant volcanic eruption. A quick internet search can point you to them over the decades and centuries. For a recent example: The 1991 eruption of Mount Pinatubo cooled global temperatures for about 2–3 years.

The chart below is taken from the Smithsonian Institute. It shows the "Known" historically active volcanoes from the 1400s to today. The chart shows clear evidence of active volcanoes increasing. However, I do not want to misrepresent the data. Over time as the population spreads out over the earth and we can better observe and report on volcanic activity because of our advancing technologies, our recorded observations will be higher. This does not mean there has not been a significant increase in active volcanoes. It means we should exercise caution when quoting representative numbers as below.

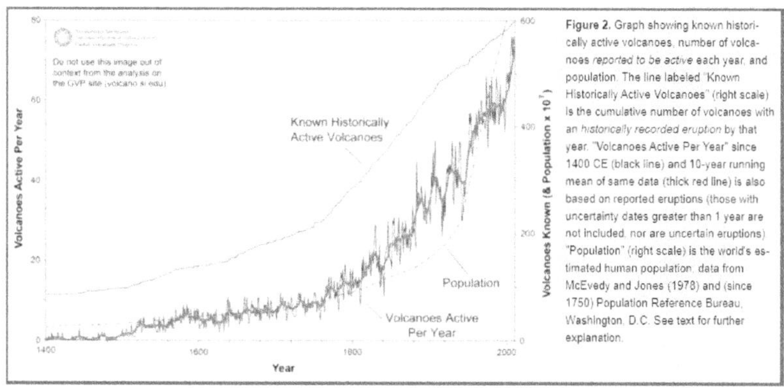

Figure 2. Graph showing known historically active volcanoes, number of volcanoes reported to be active each year, and population. The line labeled "Known Historically Active Volcanoes" (right scale) is the cumulative number of volcanoes with an historically recorded eruption by that year. "Volcanoes Active Per Year" since 1400 CE (black line) and 10-year running mean of same data (thick red line) is also based on reported eruptions (those with uncertainty dates greater than 1 year are not included, nor are uncertain eruptions). "Population" (right scale) is the world's estimated human population, data from McEvedy and Jones (1978) and (since 1750) Population Reference Bureau, Washington, D.C. See text for further explanation.

In one way or another, the Puppets attempt to point to global warming as the cause of the increases we see in natural disasters. Starting with their flawed premisses, they then begin to propagate their fear campaigns. The natural disasters we have listed cause the effects we defined at the beginning of the chapter, being: drought, famine, pestilence, plague, species in distress, shoreline erosion and human death.

Each one of these effects can and is caused by natural disasters. Where they go wrong is placing climate change as the culprit. For one example, they tell us drought results from climate change. They will then go on to say that the stress loads on the Earth's crust from periods of drought can be a significant cause of earthquakes. Now there is a stretch, to say the least.

So what does the Bible have to say about natural disasters and why they are part of our existence here on this planet we call home. In the chapter titled "In The Beginning," we extensively covered the fall of man and the resulting curse God placed on the Earth as a result of our disobedience and sin. The Earth went from a paradise to a place of constant decay leading to its eventual destruction. Although God's pronounced judgements are severe, they do not mean God does not remain in complete control of his creation. He does. God sustains well-being and creates calamity according to His will and purpose.

(Isaiah 45:7)
"The One forming light and creating darkness,
Causing well-being and creating calamity;
I am the Lord who does all these."

The third pronouncement of the judgements from God begins by focusing on the sin of Adam. Like Eve, He too had eaten from the forbidden fruit of the tree of the knowledge of good and evil. As a result, we might expect that he would also be cursed like the serpent or Satan. Instead, something surprising happens. The ground of Earth is cursed—not the man! To me, this is unexpected but a reality of God's actions.

The land has done nothing to deserve this curse; the Earth is not the culprit but the innocent victim. The curse on the Earth has consequences for humankind, but it appears the Earth suffers innocently. The task of working with the ground is now more arduous, 'thorns and thistles will appear, and humans will eat from the 'plants of the field' rather than fruit from the garden's trees. The land, however, suffers because of what humans have done. This Earth bears the curse of God.

As part of the curse, the Earth now groans as in childbearing and has been subjected to frustration and futility. The Earth now moans in a constant state of decay, awaiting the final intervention of God, who will ultimately free it and purge it through fire. Ultimately God will replace the heavens and this Earth as he will replace our bodies with a new glorified body in our renewing and glorification.

(2 Peter 3:10)
"But the day of the Lord will come like a thief, and then the heavens will vanish with a [mighty and thunderous] roar, and the [material] elements will be destroyed with intense heat, and the earth and the works that are on it will be burned up." (AMP)

(Romans 8:19-23)
"For [even the whole] creation [all nature] waits eagerly for the children of God to be revealed. For the creation was subjected to frustration and futility, not willingly [because of some intentional fault on its part], but by the will of Him who subjected it, in hope that the creation itself will also be freed from its bondage to decay [and gain entrance] into the glorious freedom of the children of God. For we know that the whole creation has been moaning together as in the pains of childbirth until now. And not only this, but we too, who have the first fruits of the Spirit joyful indication of the blessings to come], even we groan inwardly, as we wait eagerly for [the sign of] our adoption as sons—the redemption and transformation of our body [at the resurrection]." (AMP)

The prophet Isaiah also helps to describe the state of the Earth and its ultimate doom. It is wearing out like a garment and will vanish like smoke. God is the one who controls all aspects of what goes on here on earth and in the heavens. As we march towards his return, the sending and intensifying of natural disasters are His to send and His to control. Once again, we have no say in the matter, and the Puppets have no say in the matter. Events will continue along God's set course. No interventions, restrictions or Puppeteering will change or alter the path God has predestined for the Earth and for each of us.

(Isaiah 51:6)
"Lift up your eyes to the heavens, look at the earth beneath; the heavens will vanish like smoke, the earth will wear out like a garment and its inhabitants die like flies. But my salvation will last forever, my righteousness will never fail."

(Nehemiah 9:6)
"You alone are the Lord. You have made the heavens, the heaven of heavens with all their host, the earth and all that is on it, the seas and all that is in them. You give life to all of them. And the heavenly host bows down before You."

THE RISKS ARE REAL

What we are witnessing with our world today can and should undoubtedly be mind-numbing. It is a simple fact that as we march through time, every day seems to hold more devastation than the previous one. The birthing pains and groans of the Earth become louder and louder, and each event contributes to more pain and suffering as it unfolds. Each event holds its own misery for those affected by it. These events will only worsen over time.

As natural disasters increase, so do the conditions they cause. We have increasing events that directly affect our health or put our lives at risk, like drought, famine, plague or disease. Other events like pestilence, floods, rising ocean levels, shoreline erosion, and the environment we live in threaten our food resources, habitat, and mobility.

These events are a reality and can be devastating to all of us. Although they are increasing in intensity and severity, unlike the natural disasters that cause them, we can mitigate the risk and lessen the impact they impose on us. We will investigate what this should look like in the next chapter. Rather than spending their time and your money trying to fix events the Puppets have no control over, the natural disasters themselves, they should be spending their time and effort lessening the impact the natural disasters have on humanity. Now that would be worth their time and effort, and we all would be better off because of it. Unfortunately, there is no financial gain or reward in helping your fellow man. It also does not help that their hearts and motives are evil to the core.

(2 Timothy 3:13)
"while evildoers and impostors will go from bad to worse, deceiving and being deceived."

It has not been the intent of this book to discount these events or their severity. They are real. The effects and devastation of them are real. The pain and suffering they cause are real. The intent is to demonstrate that the causes are not what the Puppets are telling you and that their proposed solutions will not correct any of these problems. As we looked at in a previous chapter, their proposed solutions are more problematic than the status quo.

I am, again, not suggesting we should not do anything. We should and must but not for the reason of saving the planet; it is on its way out. We should be taking action and correcting our ways because God expects more from us. We rape this planet of sustainable resources that we do not replace for the next generations. We pollute the land, the atmosphere, and the oceans without a second thought. We consume non-renewable resources at a breakneck pace without finding feasible alternatives.

We are the stewards of the Earth, and God has given us dominion over it and the responsibility to care for it. We are failing His directives to oversee and be good caretakers of this planet we call home. We mismanage our activities and affairs and need to make a change. We will also examine what that should look like coming up in the next chapter.

God has some pretty harsh words for those that destroy this planet and will deal with them harshly when the day of judgement comes. Having dominion over the Earth does not give us a blank slate to use and abuse it for self-serving agendas and profit. God holds the deed to the Earth and is our landlord. As any landlord would expect, we should be leaving the Earth just as we found it when our time here is over. The following tenants, our children and our children's children would expect and deserve no less.

(Revelation 11:18)
"The nations were angry, and your wrath has come. The time has come for judging the dead, and for rewarding your servants the prophets and your people who revere your name, both great and small—and for destroying those who destroy the earth."

If the earthly bound events were not enough, we now believe we must face the inherent risks from our atmosphere and the solar system. These perceived risks are not new; however, with our advancing technologies and the development of new measuring and monitoring devices, they have become apparent to us. One hundred years ago, we were none the wiser. We had yet to propel ourselves or our measuring equipment into space, nor did we have the high-powered telescopes and monitoring devices we do today.

What our technology has done for us is to show us how precarious our living situation really is. We now know we live on the shell of an egg, with a hole in its atmosphere, hurtling through space at breakneck speeds surrounded by all manner of nefarious objects and events that could snuff us out in an instant. Well, that sounds encouraging.

Fortunately, for those who know the one true God, we understand he created our planet and the universe and all that is in it, including you and me. God gave us breath and placed our spirits within us. God is our father and creator and loves each one of us intimately. He even knows every hair on our heads. We also know God put our planet exactly where He wanted it to be. God holds it in the exact place He put it, and it will stay there until He is done with it or decides to move or replace it, as with everything else in His creation.

(Luke 12:7)

"Indeed the very hairs of your head are all numbered. Do not be afraid; you are far more valuable than many sparrows."

(Isaiah 42:5)

"Thus says God the Lord,
Who created the heavens and stretched them out,
Who spread out the earth and its offspring,
Who gives breath to the people on it
And spirit to those who walk in it,"

(Job 26:7)

"He stretches out the north over empty space
And hangs the earth on nothing."

When the ungodly, those who reject or do not know God, start to understand how precarious this life is and how their continuing existence hangs on 1 billion or more things going correctly all at the same time, how could they not cower in fear? One mishap, one wayward asteroid, one planet spinning out of its orbit, one galaxy careening into ours, and once again, it's game over. How could they not look for solutions to what they perceive the problems are?

God has built into us an eternal desire to live. The ungodly have this same internal desire built into them. They do not need unattainable solutions to mitigate natural disasters or climate change. They need a repentant heart and a relationship with their creator. Then, and only then, will they understand God is in charge, and their planet is not going anywhere under His leadership.

So, what are these new discoveries of potential perceived disasters we now know we face from our solar system and the stars? Starting with our atmosphere, they tell us there is a hole in our ozone layer. Ok, should we care would be the first question. We did not know we had an ozone layer until 1913, when French physicists Charles Fabry and Henri Buisson made the discovery. These two physicists determined that the ozone layer absorbs most of the Sun's ultraviolet radiation.

The ozone layer contains about ten parts per million of ozone, while the lower atmosphere only contains about .3 parts per million. That is not a lot of parts per million, but they tell us it is effective at doing its job. Ozone (O3) is a pale blue gas molecule composed of three oxygen atoms. Ozone is formed naturally through the interaction of solar ultraviolet (UV) radiation with molecular oxygen (O2), meaning it is a self-renewing resource. The majority of ozone is produced over the tropics and is transported towards the poles by stratospheric wind patterns. The ozone layer absorbs 97 to 99 percent of the Sun's medium-frequency ultraviolet light, which otherwise would potentially damage exposed life forms near the surface.

When they tell us there is a hole developing in the ozone layer, it is not an actual hole but a thinning of the layer. It has also been discovered that the thickness of the ozone layer varies worldwide and is generally thinner near the equator and thicker near the poles and varies from season to season. These variations are due to atmospheric circulation patterns and solar intensity.

The reduction of ozone in the upper atmosphere can allow an increase of UV-B radiation from the sun to reach us. The radiation can be harmful to the skin and is the leading cause of sunburn; excessive exposure can also cause cataracts and result in problems such as skin cancer. Chlorofluorocarbons or CFCs have been blamed for thinning the ozone layer and subsequently banned in most but not all countries. CFCs are found in aerosol can spray and refrigerants.

It sounds like the ozone layer is paramount and that God has created it for a very specific purpose and our benefit, you know, to keep us alive. While the 2021 Antarctic ozone hole is larger than average, it is substantially smaller than those in the late 1990s and early 2000s. Does the ozone layer naturally fluctuate over extended periods of time? Given we only have a little over 100 years of data, we do not know. However, if it follows all other weather patterns and cycles, my guess would be yes.

Given that ozone is a self-generating gas, it fluctuates from area to area, season to season, and replenishes itself as a naturally occurring gas; one would assume we are not at the life on earth ending risk they tell us. I am also confident that if God sees a need to replenish the ozone with a breath or a word, He will do so. Always keep in mind God sustains all things for His purposes and will.

(Psalm 104:30)
"You send forth Your Spirit, they are created; And You renew the face of the ground."

In the last couple of years, reports have surfaced about a wobble in the Earth as it spins on its axes; fitting enough, they have coined this wobble an Earth Wobble. Dire predictions of our ultimate doom were once again shouted from the rooftops. Predictions coming in ranged from our planet breaking free from our orbit and careening off into space to the dawn of the next ice age or, on the other side of the scale, global warming to the point of extinction of all life on earth. Of course, it was reported that global warming was the cause of this wobble.

You can find many conflicting reports on how climate change affects the Earth's wobble. Some will tell you it is because of droughts, the melting of the polar ice caps - glacial melting, or even glacial rebound. Others contend it is because of the continental drift, or mantle convection, which is the moving and shifting of the tectonic plates in the Earth's mantle. Some will say it is all of the above, adding even more causes to the list. It is enough to make your head spin – pardon the pun.

It turns out we have known about this Earth wobble since it was discovered in the late 1800s by the American astronomer Seth Carlo Chandler. Every six to fourteen years, the spin axis wobbles about 20 to 60 inches either east or west of its general drift direction. It is a common misperception that the Earth is a perfect sphere. In actual fact, it is an oblate spheroid, meaning it is elliptical rather than circular, and its rotation causes it to swell at the equator.

The earth has an uneven landmass distribution throughout its geography and a varying thickness of crust throughout its topography; think of mountains and valleys. Oceans and their tides ebb and flow with the lunar cycles creating an uneven and moving weight distribution of water on the Earth. This ebb and flow redistributes the weight of the water to different regions at different times with these tidal events. With the varied topographies contributing to the uneven distribution of landmass and the movement of water, it makes logical sense, based on physics, that a wobble exits as the Earth spins on its axis.

Consider a couple of real-life examples. When you put new tires on your car, they first go in for a balancing. The mechanic adds weights to different areas of the rim to put the tires in balance when they spin. A set of balanced tires run smooth and true on the road. If your tires are out of balance, what happens? They wobble, and you can feel your car shaking. The Earth is out of balance; it wobbles.

Or, consider a bucket of water. Suppose you place a full bucket of water on a wagon and try to pull it from here to there on an uneven surface. In that case, it will slosh back and forth, creating an uneven weight distribution, spilling some, and possibly even tipping the bucket over. Our oceans experience this same sloshing motion from high tide to low tide.

Scientists have recently discovered that the earth is not the only wobbler in our solar system. It turns out Mars is also a wobbler. Measurements over nearly two decades by spacecraft orbiting Mars uncovered that on the surface, the planet's poles wander from the average axis of rotation, with a repeated cycle of about 207 days. I am pretty sure the fear mongers will have a hard time attributing the Mars wobble to humankind-induced climate change or activities considering Elon Musk is not living there yet. He has not even had the chance to visit his new home. If I were a betting man, I would bet the other planets do some wobbling as well.

Based on all of the evidence listed above, I will assume the Earth has been a wobbler since God created it, and its wobbling ways are part of God's grand design. It makes more sense that the Earth does wobble than if it did not, given its composition and the fluidity of its elements. If this wobbling happens to become extreme, once again, I have complete confidence in God. If He needs to set the Earth straight or stop it from wobbling, he will do so with a flick of His finger. If climate change czars tell you they are concerned about the

Earth wobble and that we are causing it, tell them to worry about their own brain wobble before they bother you with this nonsense.

The next big item on the hit list of extinction-level events is the dreaded killer asteroid or comet slamming into the Earth. We are not talking about the small stones you see frequently lighting up the sky as they penetrate the atmosphere and careen towards Earth, the ones with the spectacular light trails that burn up as they descend towards the ground. No, we are talking about the granddaddy of them all, the city-sized planet killer.

This granddaddy of an asteroid is the stuff of legends. Hollywood has been producing world-ending asteroid collision movies since the 1950s with "The Day the Sky Exploded." We are not talking about b-movies or direct to DVD movies, but Hollywood blockbusters, and they continue to throw them at us – pardon the pun, again. The latest hot release as of the writing of this book is "Don't Look Up." Add Armageddon, Meteor, Night of the Comet, Greenland, Asteroid, The Good Dinosaur, Seeking a Friend for the End of

The World, Home Threatened, Deep Impact, and the list goes on. We are obsessed with the possibility of extinction by a space rock. In his final book, Brief Answers to the Big Questions, Physicist Stephen Hawking considered an asteroid collision to be the biggest threat to the planet.

The U.S. Congress has declared that the general welfare and security of the United States requires that NASA be directed to detecting, tracking, cataloguing, and characterizing near-Earth asteroids and comets to provide warning and mitigation of the potential hazard. In obedience to Congress, NASA is developing methods for asteroid collision prevention.

Developing these systems can only mean they believe we are actually at risk of this happening rather than being just a hypothetical. One example is the space agency's Double Asteroid Redirection Test (DART) mission, which launched in November 2021. The DART mission is sending a spacecraft crashing into an asteroid at speeds of approximately 15,000 mph to test if we can successfully alter the trajectory of a space rock.

China is also developing its own asteroid defection system. At China's National Space Science Center, researchers found in simulations that 23 Long March 5 rockets simultaneously hitting an asteroid could deflect its original path by a distance 1.4 times the Earth's radius. Chinese researchers want to send more than 20 of China's largest rockets to practice turning away a sizable asteroid in the near future. I wonder if China and the US got their ideas from the movies? It would not be the first time.

Although I have been rather tough on the Puppets throughout this book, I guess I should probably give them one win. They can have this one; they nailed it. I can say with 100 percent certainty that an extinction-level event asteroid or comet will impact the earth along with a host of other heavenly objects.

How do I know this? God is sending one in His time, and He has even given it a name. God has named the planet's nemesis Wormwood and describes it as a great star hurtled to the Earth by

His third angel during the upcoming tribulation period. Considering God names all of His stars in the galaxies, it is no surprise that this one has a name also. I am sure the Puppets would be cringing if they knew they were aligning themselves with God's Word. I am guessing it was not intentional, but good for them.

(Revelation 8:7-12)
"The first angel blew his trumpet, and there followed hail and fire, mixed with blood, and these were thrown upon the earth. And a third of the earth was burned up, and a third of the trees were burned up, and all green grass was burned up."

"The second angel blew his trumpet, and something like a great mountain, burning with fire, was thrown into the sea, and a third of the sea became blood. A third of the living creatures in the sea died, and a third of the ships were destroyed."

"The third angel blew his trumpet, and a great star fell from heaven, blazing like a torch, and it fell on a third of the rivers and on the springs of water. The name of the star is Wormwood. A third of the waters became wormwood, and

many people died from the water, because it had been made bitter."

"The fourth angel blew his trumpet, and a third of the sun was struck, and a third of the moon, and a third of the stars, so that a third of their light might be darkened, and a third of the day might be kept from shining, and likewise a third of the night." (ESV)

If there is one thing I know, even with all of their valiant efforts, the governments or their militaries will have no success in deflecting the Wormwood star when it arrives. I don't care how many rockets they explode, spacecraft they fly into it, or asteroid deflecting witch dances they do; they are wasting their time and your money. God's will and purpose will not be thwarted or turned aside. Wormwood will arrive on time and deliver God's foreordained and intended results according to His will and purpose.

You have probably noticed throughout this book and, in particular, these last couple of chapters that I have not included citations to fill up twenty pages of an index for the information I am providing. I do not need to bolster my word count. There is more information to go over than I could possibly write. This has been intentional. My goal has not been to either prove or disprove natural disasters, the consequences of natural disasters, or potential cosmic events. We know they occur and are occurring with greater intensity and frequency by a simple internet search and that new perceived risks are being realized. You can do the research as quickly as I have. Sending you on a bunch of citation searches would be a waste of your time and defeat the book's purpose.

My intended purpose is threefold. First, I am attempting to communicate the genuine threat we face today. This threat does not come from any of the above three categories. These events and the consequences of the events are not going anywhere. The actual danger comes from those who are telling you otherwise and that they have the solution. Those hypocritical Puppets who distort, lie, fabricate, misdirect and exaggerate risk through fear-mongering and falsehoods. They do this to exert their will and purpose on you and execute their globalist agendas while stripping you of your civil and religious liberties and way of life.

My second purpose is to encourage you to test everything you are being told against common sense and reasonableness – to employ critical thinking and sound judgement. If something looks, smells, and tastes like bat guano, it probably is bat guano. It is starting to come to many people's attention that something untoward and bordering on just plain crazy is going on. The true agenda of this supposed "Great Reset" is starting to come to light and what is being illuminated is the pure evil intent and globalist plans of these Godless perpetrators. Open your eyes and smell the guano. Don't let yourself be led like sheep to the slaughter. Know what is coming and prepare yourself for it as we will explore next.

My third purpose is to Highlight and emphasize the infallible, inspired, unfailing, unerring truth of God's word. We need to look no further than the scripture to understand where this world is heading and what season it is heading there. We will explore this in the last chapter of the book. The Puppets are clueless about the truth of scripture and do not understand the impotence and ultimate cost of their planning and scheming. They will ultimately get their globalizing agenda accomplished only to have it snuffed out along with themselves by our Lord Jesus Christ when he returns to claim his throne.

WHERE DO I FIT

As we go through our daily lives, each of us has two areas of fundamental interaction. We interact with our relationships with God and each other, which I call the societal side of the ledger. We interact with our surroundings, environment and planet, which I call the ecological side of the ledger. These interactions are affected in different ways by both internal choice and external influences resulting in either positive, neutral, or negative outcomes.

On the societal side of the ledger, the Christian has up to seven hierarchal relationships that we manage each day. Our first relationship is with God, followed by our spouse, biological family, Christian Family, local church, Kingdom church, and the world. The list is considerably smaller for the unsaved, consisting of a spouse, biological family, and the world. Of course, if neither group has a spouse, cross that one off the list. Only when you have a deep loving relationship with God will your other relationships be healthy. God comes first.

As this world goes through the rapid change we are currently experiencing, our relationships get tested in ways we could never have imagined even five years ago. People are lining up on opposite sides of the issues and digging in. The governments, elitists, and scientists drive a deep wedge between both sides. They do this through media control, propaganda, and the suppression of free speech, with social media censoring all opposing viewpoints. They fuel the divisions and vilify anyone who does not align with or fall into step with their narrative. We now see families, places of employment, and even churches, split and divided, with one side pitted against the other with dire consequences and outcomes.

None of what we see should surprise the faithful Born Again Christian as we are told in scripture precisely what will happen in the end days. We are witnessing the scriptures being fulfilled before our very eyes. The divisions we are seeing and the perversity of the nations and people are precursors to the rapture and, ultimately, the seven-year tribulation. We live in scary but exciting times, knowing God's return is imminent.

The rapture is the removal of the restrainer, or Holy Spirit, and the church from this world. The tribulation is the seven-year period where God exercises His judgement on this perverse and unrepentant generation ending in the return of Jesus Christ to set up His Kingdom and to judge the nations.

(2 Timothy 3:1-10)
"But mark this: There will be terrible times in the last days. People will be lovers of themselves, lovers of money, boastful, proud, abusive, disobedient to their parents, ungrateful, unholy, without love, unforgiving, slanderous, without self-control, brutal, not lovers of the good, treacherous, rash, conceited, lovers of pleasure rather than lovers of God—having a form of godliness but denying its power. Have nothing to do with such people."

"They are the kind who worm their way into homes and gain control over gullible women, who are loaded down with sins and are swayed by all kinds of evil desires, always learning but never able to come to a knowledge of the truth. Just as Jannes and Jambres opposed Moses, so also these teachers oppose the truth. They are men of depraved minds, who, as

far as the faith is concerned, are rejected. But they will not get very far because, as in the case of those men, their folly will be clear to everyone."

(Luke 12:52-53)
"From now on there will be five in one family divided against each other, three against two and two against three. 53 They will be divided, father against son and son against father, mother against daughter and daughter against mother, mother-in-law against daughter-in-law and daughter-in-law against mother-in-law."

This book deals with the ecological side of the ledger. My upcoming and companion book to this one, titled "Tribulation Training – Goats to the Left, Sheep to the Right" is an in-depth expose on the societal side of our ledger. The book walks the reader through an in-depth study of where we are, where we are going, how we will get there, and when. It deals with each of our relationships, the rapture, the tribulation and the coming Kingdom of Christ. For the purpose of this current book, we will continue with the ecological side of the ledger where our focus has been.

We are left wondering where we fit in and what we should do as this new world unfolds before us at breakneck speed. Should we join the Puppet cheering bandwagon and support the ushering in of "The Great Reset," ignoring our convictions and blindly accepting the lies and deceit? Or, should we sit in opposition to evil scheming and seek to overthrow the governments and their agendas to impose our will and purpose in replacement of the globalist's agenda?

The answer is none of the above. We are admonished in the scriptures not to love the things of this world, be of it, or be conformed to it because Satan controls it: it is his domain. This world is a temporary home as we await Heaven and ultimately the new Heaven and Earth. We are not to align with or have anything to do with evil or those perpetuating it, and certainly, we are to have nothing to do with any instruction that contradicts the teaching of the Bible.

(2 Timothy 3:16-17)
"All Scripture is breathed out by God and profitable for teaching, for reproof, for correction, and for training in

righteousness, that the man of God may be complete, equipped for every good work." (ESV)

(1 John 5:19)
"We know that we are from God, and the whole world lies in the power of the evil one." (ESV)

We are to live for Christ and spread the Gospel. We can only share it when we know it. You would be amazed at how many professing Christians do not read their Bible on a daily basis. We should not try to fit in or act how people of this world act. Rather instead, we are to be imitators of Christ and spread the gospel so others will come to know Him and join us in our heavenly home one day. We accomplish this through our words, actions, works, Holy living, and letting our light shine in this perverse and crooked generation.

In surveys conducted about why people shy away from or reject Christianity, one of the prominent answers is because of the hypocrisy they see in those professing to be Christians. Hypocrisy is the practice of engaging in the same behaviour or activity for which one criticizes another or the practice of claiming to have moral standards or beliefs to which one's own behaviour does not conform to or exhibit. Today's entertaining, watered-down, compromising church is full of hypocrites keeping people from knowing our Lord Jesus Christ and His saving grace. In my previous book, "REALLY? What's Gone Wrong and Why - How Not to Read the Bible" I covered this topic in-depth.

(John 17:14-16)
"I have given them your word, and the world has hated them because they are not of the world, just as I am not of the world. I do not ask that you take them out of the world, but that you keep them from the evil one. They are not of the world, just as I am not of the world." (ESV)

(John 15:19)
"If you were of the world, the world would love you as its own; but because you are not of the world, but I chose you out of the world, therefore the world hates you." (ESV)

(1 John 4:5)
"They are from the world; therefore they speak from the world, and the world listens to them." (ESV)

"You are the light of the world. A city set on a hill cannot be hidden. Nor do people light a lamp and put it under a basket, but on a stand, and it gives light to all in the house. In the same way, let your light shine before others, so that they may see your good works and give glory to your Father who is in heaven." (ESV)

So, the question was, should we join the Puppet cheering bandwagon and outwardly support their march to globalization and the suppression of the population, including you and me? The resounding answer is no unless you want to join the Devils team and do his work and bidding. We pointed out earlier that there are only two teams, Gods and Satan's. If you are not for God, you are against Him as taught in the scriptures. The Puppets are the leaders of the other team—the bad guys. We are to have nothing to do with Satan's lies and deceit. How do we know they are the Bad guys? We know because they are both Godless God-haters and spew lies and deceit, just like their father, the Devil.

(John 8:44)

"You belong to your father, the devil, and you want to carry out your father's desires. He was a murderer from the beginning, not holding to the truth, for there is no truth in him. When he lies, he speaks his native language, for he is a liar and the father of lies."

Also, as mentioned in a previous chapter, God has a plan that has been laid out since the beginning of creation. It is the plan for our redemption and renewal for both the child of God and His creation. This planet and solar system are a temporary home in a constant state of decay and depredation and will one day cease to exist. The Puppets will not save it with all their valiant efforts, nor will you. Your efforts would be futile and in vain.

God's plan and purpose will not be thwarted, delayed or altered in any way. Global warming or any of the other planet-ending "disasters" and the consequences of those disasters we have looked at in this book will not derail God's plans or alter them in any way. A cosmic event will not end our existence as we know it until God sends Wormwood to pay us a visit. We will continue to experience these disasters and their effects in increasing intensity and severity. Life will march on, just as it has, until the church is raptured, and the four horsemen of the apocalypse are sent to the four corners of the earth to kick off the tribulation.

(Matthew 24:37-39)
For as were the days of Noah, so will be the coming of the Son of Man. For as in those days before the flood they were eating and drinking, marrying and giving in marriage, until the day when Noah entered the ark, and they were unaware until the flood came and swept them all away, so will be the coming of the Son of Man.

Stick to your God-given job of sharing the Gospel and resisting evil. Share it with all who are willing to listen, even with those who will not. Resist evil and live Holy and blameless before God in a manner pleasing to Him. Let your light shine, and your Godly example be a witness to others. Develop a deep relationship with God and his word through reading, prayer, meditating on the Word, and fellowshipping with those of like mind. Preach the word in season and out as the scriptures admonish us to do and be ready for the glorious appearing of our Lord Jesus Christ.

(2 Timothy 4:2)
"preach the word [as an official messenger]; be ready when the time is right and even when it is not [keep your sense of urgency, whether the opportunity seems favorable or unfavorable, whether convenient or inconvenient, whether welcome or unwelcome]; correct [those who err in doctrine or behavior], warn [those who sin], exhort and encourage [those who are growing toward spiritual maturity], with inexhaustible patience and [faithful] teaching." (AMP)

The next question is, should there be a revolt or movement against the government. Once again, the answer is a resounding no. There is a raging debate going on right now within the Christian circles on how we should react to the ongoing and worsening government overreach and the stripping of our civil and religious rights. On the one hand, people advocate civil disobedience, unrest, and even violence in some cases. On the other hand, you have folks supporting everything the governments are mandating and telling you we need to fully comply because it is what the scriptures teach, taking God's word both out of context and misapplying it.

How do we reconcile with either side? The answer is we do not. Our actions and reactions should be somewhere in the middle of the two polarizing positions and always Christ-centered. We should be asking ourselves what Jesus would do or expect from us in all circumstances. All of our reactions and actions need to be pleasing to Him and Biblically derived. If we are engaging in anything that Christ would be frowning upon, we should not be doing it. In no place in the New Testament do we find instructions or examples to overthrow or usurp the government. In actuality, the scriptures teach the exact opposite.

The disciples believed that Jesus had come to set up His Kingdom during His time with them. They were prepared to install him to power by force if necessary, not understanding His time had not yet come. When they came to arrest Jesus in the garden, Peter looped off the ear of Malchus, the High Priests servant, and was prepared to cut them all down. Jesus told him to stand down; His work had not yet been completed. He also makes it clear that if God wanted to deal with these men by force, He could call on legions of angels to do his bidding. He did not require Peter's sword, nor does he require yours.

A time will come to stand up to evil by force. Jesus will lead that time at his second coming with his legion of angels with His Bride in tow. Our job is not to attempt to disrupt governments by force or instill our will on them between now and then. They are serving God's purpose of marching us to His return. Our job is to preach the word.

(Matthew 26:51-54)
"With that, one of Jesus' companions reached for his sword, drew it out and struck the servant of the high priest, cutting off his ear. "Put your sword back in its place," Jesus said to him, "for all who draw the sword will die by the sword. Do you think I cannot call on my Father, and he will at once put at my disposal more than twelve legions of angels? But how then would the Scriptures be fulfilled that say it must happen in this way?"

God appoints governments and their leaders for his purpose and time. Suppose we apply a little logic to try to understand why these evil people are in power; we all of a sudden gain a little clarity. We know that as we march towards the end, a global leader will rise up who is given global authority over all nations by Satan. The name given to us is the Antichrist. It only makes sense that the countries' leaders who will give up their national power and sovereignty to the Antichrist are probably weak-willed sycophants willing to hand their authority over to Satan's man of the hour.

Maybe God will allow a senile old man with clear signs of dementia into the office of the President for His purpose. He might even appoint an ex-bartending ski-bum playboy into the office of the Prime Minister with no apparent abilities to run a country, to be led around by the nose by the global elitists and those who are intent on evil. One never knows.

(Romans 13:1)

"Let everyone be subject to the governing authorities, for there is no authority except that which God has established. The authorities that exist have been established by God."

Two good examples of God appointing evil leaders to accomplish His purposes are Pharaoh and Nebuchadnezzar. An excellent example of God appointing an inept, unqualified leader was Saul, whose primary job before taking power was good-looking "Donkey Finder." There should be no surprise to us when we look at who God has in power today in countries worldwide.

So, should we be attempting to usurp power from these God-appointed men? No, we should not. We should certainly be exercising our right to vote and not supporting tyranny with our contributions or speech, but rising up against them is not the answer. God has them there for a purpose. Who are we to question God's choices? The existing authorities have been established and appointed by God as the scriptures teach.

On the other side of the fence, you have the capitulators in all things—those who follow every rule, restriction, and edict perfectly without wavering right or left. Just like we should not be seeking to overthrow leadership by force, nor should we be bowing down to the government when they attempt to replace God's authority with their own. God is the ultimate authority. His authority supersedes every other authority on Earth, including the governments.

The capitulators will quote scripture without understanding what they are quoting or its actual meaning and teaching. We will have to get into a little Greek for this but stick with me. We find examples of disobedience to the governing authorities that God condones throughout the scriptures. How do we know God condones them? Because Jesus himself was one of them by teaching against the instructions of the religious rulers of the day not to. We find these examples throughout both the Old and New Testaments. We will look at a couple of examples selected from hundreds.

Moses would not have been alive to accomplish God's purposes if the folks of the day did not go against the government mandate. Pharaoh ordered that the midwives kill all newborn Hebrew boys to keep them from growing up and becoming soldiers.

Rahab directly disobeyed a command from the king of Jericho to produce the Israelite spies who had entered the city to gain intelligence for battle. She was redeemed from the city's destruction when Joshua and the Israeli army destroyed it.

King Saul decreed no one could eat until Saul had won his battle with the Philistines. Saul's son Jonathan ate honey to refresh himself from the army's battle. When Saul found out about it, he ordered his son to die. The people resisted Saul and saved Jonathan from being put to death

Queen Jezebel was killing God's prophets. Obadiah took a hundred of them and hid them from her. Ahaziah began to destroy the royal offspring of the house of Judah. Joash was taken by the king's daughter and hidden to preserve the bloodline. Jehoiada declared Joash to be king six years later and put Athaliah to death. Shadrach, Meshach and Abednego refused to bow down to the golden idol in disobedience to King Nebuchadnezzar's command, and we know how that story went. We could look at hundreds more.

In the New Testament, the religious authorities continually commanded the disciples to stop teaching about Jesus. Of course, they continued unto death and martyrdom.

King Herod arrested some believers, including James and Peter, and put them on public trial. The night before the trial, an angel of the Lord woke Peter up, removed his chains, opened the prison doors, and led him out the prison's main gate. After the jailbreak, Peter went on to write in 1 Peter:

(1 Peter 2:13-14)
"Submit yourselves for the Lord's sake to every human authority: whether to the emperor, as the supreme authority, or to governors, who are sent by him to punish those who do wrong and to commend those who do right."

When Paul was in Damascus, he escaped from a city governor trying to arrest him by concealing himself in a wicker basket and having himself lowered down the city wall through a window. Afterwards, Paul wrote:

(Romans 13:1)
"Let everyone be subject to the governing authorities, for there is no authority except that which God has established. The authorities that exist have been established by God."

Are Paul, Peter and the other disciples hypocrites? Are we dealing with a conflict in scripture? Absolutely not on either account. The key to understanding is in the word "submit." The Greek word hupo-tasso, is translated as "submit" or "be subject to." It means to arrange stuff respectfully in an orderly manner underneath. This word is used in Ephesians 5:22 to encourage husbands and wives to submit to one another, demonstrating God's concern for order and respect. Paul and Peter teach that governing authorities are necessary for keeping peace and order.

In the New Testament Greek, to submit does not always mean to obey! They are two separate actions or postures and words. Peter and Paul could have used the word hupo-kouo translated "obey," but they did not. They chose the word hupo-tasso. Used twenty-one times in the New Testament, hupo-kouo always suggests a hierarchical context used in the relationship between parents and children of slaves and masters. (Eph 6:1 and 6:5).

Although Paul, Peter, the other followers of Jesus, and Old Testament characters deliberately disobeyed laws that conflicted with God's commands, they still submitted to the authorities by accepting the legal consequences of their actions. The first people who sought to worship Jesus, the wise men from the East, deliberately disobeyed the orders of King Herod to tell him where Jesus was, a criminal offence punishable by death.

As Christians, the law cannot be our moral guide. Slavery was lawful, the holocaust was lawful, abortion is lawful, keeping people from meeting together in church is now lawful in some places. Speaking scriptural truth is soon to be unlawful. On and on and on. God is our ultimate authority, and we are to obey his commands above the commands of the government when they conflict with or attempt to supersede our instructions from the scriptures, as we see in our scriptural examples above. Simply put, the law does not dictate our ethics. God does, and it is His authority we submit to when the governments attempt to usurp that authority with rules and mandates that contradict the scriptures.

We would have a tough time performing baptisms, anointing with oil and laying on hands in prayer, exercising scriptural discipline with the leadership, extending the right hand of fellowship, and the list goes on. We are told not to forsake the meeting with one another in fellowship. The government overreaches its authority when it tells us otherwise in contradiction to what God commands us.

(Hebrews 10:25)
"not forsaking our meeting together [as believers for worship and instruction], as is the habit of some, but encouraging one

another; and all the more [faithfully] as you see the day [of Christ's return] approaching." (AMP)

Using the meeting of the church as our example above, I am not advocating calling all news stations and displaying civil obedience as a badge when you decide to meet as a body in disobedience to a government order. I am conveying that God's commands supersede the governments, and if they tell you to stop meeting, meet underground and in secret.

Christians should resist a government that commands or compels evil and work non-violently within the laws of the land to change a government that permits evil. Civil disobedience is permitted when the government's laws or commands directly violate God's laws and commands. If a Christian disobeys an evil government, the Christian should accept that government's punishment for his actions if unable to flee.

The book of Acts records the civil disobedience of Peter and John towards the authorities that were in power at the time. After Peter healed a man born lame, Peter and John were arrested for preaching about Jesus and put in jail. Peters and John's response was:

(Acts 4:19-20)
"But Peter and John replied, "Which is right in God's eyes: to listen to you, or to him? You be the judges! As for us, we cannot help speaking about what we have seen and heard."

Later, the rulers confronted the apostles again and reminded them of their command not to teach about Jesus, again, Peter responded:

(Acts 5:29)
Peter and the other apostles replied: "We must obey God rather than human beings!"

GOODBYE WORLD

Throughout this book, I have used terms like "You're not going to save it," "The world is doomed," "In these last days," "The end times," and so on. These terms presuppose their own truth, but are they accurate? How do we know we are coming to the end of the world as we know it and that it will ultimately be destroyed? How do we really know we will not be able to save this planet? How do we know these are the last days? The majority of folks still believe there is hope to carry on just as we are. Unfortunately, they have a big surprise coming very soon.

There are two main questions above. Will this planet really be destroyed, and if so, when will it happen? The first question is the easy one. God says it will be, so there can be no doubt about that. We looked at the cursing of the planet back in our chapter titled "In the Beginning." The Earth began its slow death from that day onward. What is even more interesting than the Earth's "death by decay" is that God will accelerate its demise. He is not waiting until the sun burns itself out or until planetary orbits decay, hurtling the planet off into the void. No, God will be intervening to speed the timeline up.

Our Puppets have coined the term "The Great Reset," which is their vision for globalization and ushering in a one-world governing authority, currency, set of laws, and the standardization of rules and regulations. God is way ahead of them. He has already initiated his first great reset in the flood event purging this earth of the founding adulterous generations evil, with the exception of Noah and his family, who found favour in God's eyes. Gods second great reset will be by fire, bringing an end to this planet, but why and when? Step one is our salvation.

From the beginning of the biblical narrative in Genesis, God planned the redemption of fallen mankind and His cursed creation through a promised saviour. We cannot save ourselves or the planet. The Scripture narrative shows that all mankind has a sinful nature. That every inclination of the thoughts of the human heart is only evil all the time Genesis 6:5, and that all fall short of the standard of righteousness set forth by God's Holiness and His Word. Romans 3:23 tells us that "all have sinned and fallen short of the glory of God." Not only are we all sinners, but there is also a cost for our sin that we all pay, and that price is death "the wages of sin is death" from Romans 6:23.

(Genesis 6:5)
"The Lord saw how great the wickedness of the human race had become on the earth, and that every inclination of the thoughts of the human heart was only evil all the time."

(Romans 3:23)
"for all have sinned and fall short of the glory of God,"

(Romans 6:23)
"For the wages of sin is death, but the gift of God is eternal life in Christ Jesus our Lord."

God loves us and has demonstrated His love toward us, that while we were still sinners, Christ died for us. Christ came to redeem us because God loves us and sent his Son to die in our place and take our sins upon himself. Jesus Christ lived in complete righteousness and without sin. He took the sin of those who believe, nailed it to the cross, and was a sacrifice in their place so that they may have forgiveness, righteousness, and life.

Christ became our sacrifice and victory by raising from the dead and defeating death. When we believe in our hearts and confess with our mouth faith in Jesus Christ and His redemptive work, we are saved by Him through grace. Not by works lest any man boast. Salvation is a free gift from God for those who believe. Once saved by grace, we become Christ's ambassadors, as though God were making his appeal through us. Be reconciled to God. God made him who had no sin to be sin for us, so that in him we might become the righteousness of God.

(Romans 5:8)
"But God demonstrates his own love for us in this: While we were still sinners, Christ died for us."

(John 3:16)
"For God so loved the world that he gave his one and only Son, that whoever believes in him shall not perish but have eternal life."

(Romans 10:9)
"If you declare with your mouth, "Jesus is Lord," and believe in your heart that God raised him from the dead, you will be saved."

(Ephesians 2:8-9)

"For it is by grace you have been saved, through faith—and this is not from yourselves, it is the gift of God—not by works, so that no one can boast."

(1 Corinthians 15:57)

"But thanks be to God! He gives us the victory through our Lord Jesus Christ."

(2 Corinthians 5:20-21)

"We are therefore Christ's ambassadors, as though God were making his appeal through us. We implore you on Christ's behalf: Be reconciled to God. 21 God made him who had no sin to be sin[b] for us, so that in him we might become the righteousness of God."

Once saved, the Christian awaits God's imminent return and His glorious appearing. Regeneration, or the new birth, is a work of God's grace whereby believers become new creatures in Christ Jesus. It is a change of heart by the Holy Spirit through the conviction of sin. The Christian sinner responds in repentance toward God and faith in the Lord Jesus Christ. Repentance and faith are inseparable experiences of the grace of God.

The Christian becomes part of the body of Christ, His church. One day soon, Jesus Christ will come in the clouds to call the church, His bride, to meet him in the air. The bride will be taken to heaven for seven years, known as the Marriage Supper of the Lamb. The tribulation will begin on earth at this point and last for seven years. At the end of the seven years, Christ will return with his Church to bind Satan in the abyss for 1000 years, judge the nations and set up his kingdom for what is called the millennium Kingdom. At the end of the 1000 years, this disposable planet will be purged and the New Heaven and the New Earth will be created for us to dwell in for all eternity.

1 Thessalonians 4:13-18

"Brothers and sisters, we do not want you to be uninformed about those who sleep in death, so that you do not grieve like the rest of mankind, who have no hope. For we believe that Jesus died and rose again, and so we believe that God will bring with Jesus those who have fallen asleep in him. According to the Lord's word, we tell you that we who are still alive, who are left until the coming of the Lord, will certainly not precede those who have fallen asleep. For the

Lord himself will come down from heaven, with a loud command, with the voice of the archangel and with the trumpet call of God, and the dead in Christ will rise first. After that, we who are still alive and are left will be caught up together with them in the clouds to meet the Lord in the air. And so we will be with the Lord forever. Therefore encourage one another with these words."

(1 Corinthians 15:51-52)

"Listen, I tell you a mystery: We will not all sleep, but we will all be changed—in a flash, in the twinkling of an eye, at the last trumpet. For the trumpet will sound, the dead will be raised imperishable, and we will be changed."

Ok, that was a mouthful. Please know that the above commentary is my firm position on the upcoming events based on my Biblical study, holding the position of a literal dispensationalist and strong convictions of what the Word teaches. It is not the purpose of this book to defend the pre-tribulation view as above. I cover this topic with a solid Biblical defence in my upcoming book "Tribulation Training – Goats to the Left, Sheep to the Right."

Of the four main views of end-time events, Pre-Tribulation Rapture, Mid-Tribulation Rapture, Pre-Wrath Rapture, and the Post-Tribulation Rapture, the Pre-Tribulationist view is the only one that fits the narrative of scripture without having to allegorize a bunch of the text, remove the Nation of Israel from the narrative, or remove or ignore passages of the Bible altogether. If you are interested in a Biblical defence of the Pre-Tribulation position that is impossible to discount, grab the next book. If you are interested in knowing why you should read the Bible in a literal sense from a dispensationalist's viewpoint, pick up my previous book, "REALLY? What's Gone Wrong and Why – How Not to Read the Bible."

The purpose of including the above narrative of the Pre-Tribulation position is to walk us to the point of God doing away with this temporary home we call Earth and ushering in the new heaven and the new Earth. Independent of the position you hold on the rapture's timing, this planet is doomed and will be replaced. God not only has the redemptive plan in place for mankind but His created universe as well. The universe and earth will be renewed, as we see in the below scriptures.

(Revelation 21:1-7)

"Then I saw "a new heaven and a new earth," for the first heaven and the first earth had passed away, and there was no longer any sea. I saw the Holy City, the new Jerusalem, coming down out of heaven from God, prepared as a bride beautifully dressed for her husband. And I heard a loud voice from the throne saying, "Look! God's dwelling place is now among the people, and he will dwell with them. They will be his people, and God himself will be with them and be their God. He will wipe every tear from their eyes. There will be no more death or mourning or crying or pain, for the old order of things has passed away."

He who was seated on the throne said, "I am making everything new!" Then he said, "Write this down, for these words are trustworthy and true."

He said to me: "It is done. I am the Alpha and the Omega, the Beginning and the End. To the thirsty I will give water without cost from the spring of the water of life. Those who are victorious will inherit all this, and I will be their God and they will be my children."

Many Christians out there hold to the belief that the redeemed in Christ will be heading off to live eternally with God in heaven. The Bible does not teach this. Although we spend some time in heaven during the tribulation event, and probably when God recreates the world and the heavens, we do not live there throughout eternity.

John, in Revelation 21:1, writes, "I saw a new heaven and a new earth." God is going to burn up this Earth and heaven. In 2 Peter 3, We're told that He will burn away all the sin and rebelliousness attached to the Earth. He will take this earth and reshape it with fire, and out of that fiery inferno will come the new heavens and the new Earth.

The new Earth God will create for us will be refreshed and perfected to what God created before it was polluted by sin and changed by the curse. We will dwell in the New Jerusalem God brings down out of heaven to this "New Earth" he will create. The Bible teaches that we will spend eternity in new glorified bodies in a New Jerusalem on a new Earth fellowshipping with God who will dwell among us where righteousness dwells. He will be our God, and we will be his people.

(2 Peter 3:10-13)

"But the day of the Lord will come like a thief. The heavens will disappear with a roar; the elements will be destroyed by fire, and the earth and everything done in it will be laid bare. Since everything will be destroyed in this way, what kind of people ought you to be? You ought to live holy and godly lives as you look forward to the day of God and speed its coming. That day will bring about the destruction of the heavens by fire, and the elements will melt in the heat. But in keeping with his promise we are looking forward to a new heaven and a new earth, where righteousness dwells."

(2 Corinthians 6:16)

"What agreement is there between the temple of God and idols? For we are the temple of the living God. As God has said: "I will live with them and walk among them, and I will be their God, and they will be my people.""

No one knows the day or the hour when God will return for his church. If anyone tells you they know when that is, they have been deceived and are deceivers and do not know the scriptures. We are to watch and be ready for his imminent return; it could be today. We are given insight into what the season will look like, though. Matthew 24, Mark 13 and Luke 21 provide us with a glimpse along with other New Testament passages. What we see in our world today looks very familiar to what the scriptures describe this world will look like when Christ returns. Are you ready? Are you saved? If you do not know Jesus Christ as your saviour, you should seek salvation by accepting God's free gift of salvation rather than trying to save this dying disposable world.

(Matthew 24:42-44)

"Therefore keep watch, because you do not know on what day your Lord will come. But understand this: If the owner of the house had known at what time of night the thief was coming, he would have kept watch and would not have let his house be broken into. So you also must be ready, because the Son of Man will come at an hour when you do not expect him."

So, what we know without a doubt is God will sustain this planet until its purpose has been served and in His time destroys and renews it with fire. A new heaven and earth will be created, which will be our final destination and home for those who put their trust in him. The Puppets and their scheming are in vain. They are evil men following their evil hearts beholden to and following the Devil's agenda. They are Satan's workmen. We will not change God's divine plan, timetable, or ultimate destruction of this Earth no matter what they tell you and how many restrictions they saddle you with.

I have mentioned a couple of times that I am not supporting the abuse or misuse of the Earth. Our responsibility is to care for and respect the planet God has given us as our temporary home. If you believe supporting green initiatives has value, you should support them because it is the right thing to do before God. You should not be supporting them because some global elitist tells you you have to and when, but because it is the right thing to do. It is all of our responsibility to treat this earth with respect.

Acting in a responsible manner is not easy or convenient. We now live in a disposable world where we want everything at our fingertips, and we want it now. It is one of the diseases of this modern society we have built. If you genuinely want to play your part, there are many actions you can take to reduce pollution, emissions, generate less waste and consume less energy. The entirety of this book could be filled with steps you can take.

Stop using bottled water. Purchase a ceramic filter that lasts years. Consolidate trips in the car and carpool for supplies or use a bike when you can. Stop supporting companies that do not streamline packaging. Stop supporting resource gobbling billionaires who tell you do as I say, not as I do. You know, the same billionaire hypocrites at these climate conventions figuring out ways to strip you of your lifestyle and rights. Buy in bulk to reduce packaging. Turn off power-consuming devices at night. Turn the air conditioning and heat down when you are not in the house or at night when sleeping. Shop locally and support local businesses. Make a vegetable garden to grow your vegetables in the summer and for canning in the winter. You get the picture. We can all play our part in being responsible before God as we await his return.

(Job 12:7-10)
"But ask the animals, and they will teach you, or the birds in the sky, and they will tell you; or speak to the earth, and it will teach you, or let the fish in the sea inform you. Which of all these does not know that the hand of the Lord has done this? In his and is the life of every creature and the breath of all mankind."

THANK YOU

Thank you for taking the time to read this book. It is my sincere hope that you have enjoyed its content. The overarching goal of this work has been to demonstrate that God is ultimately in control of all things and to put your trust in Him.

May God richly bless and keep you until we are called to meet our Savior in the air. Amen.

If you have enjoyed this work, please consider pointing it out to others. As a new struggling author, I can use all the help I can get.

Please consider my follow-up book, which expounds on the societal side of our journey towards heaven. It is available in March of 2022 from your local Amazon.

"TRIBULATION TRAINING – Goats To The Left, Sheep To The Right"

Please also consider my previous debut Christian book, also available from your local Amazon.

"REALLY! What's Gone Wrong And Why, How Not To Read The Bible"

For current news events or weekly sermons and teaching, consider joining me on my ministry website:

www.thenarrowway.ca

I can be reached by email at:

brian@thenarrowway.ca

Your Humble Servant in Christ,

Brian Cockell

9 781777 111861